THE PATHS OF MY LIFE

A CHRISTIAN'S JOURNEY

THE PATHS OF MY LIFE

A CHRISTIAN'S JOURNEY

MARTIN L. DORNAN SR.

ARPress
ILLUMINATING IDEAS,
EMPOWERING VOICES

ARPress
45 Dan Road Suite 5
Canton MA 02021

Hotline: 1(888) 821-0229
Fax: 1(508) 545-7580

Ordering Information:
Quantity sales. Special discounts are available on quantity purchases by corporations, associations, and others. For details, contact the publisher at the address above.

Printed in the United States of America.

ISBN-13:   Softcover   979-8-89356-591-1
            eBook   979-8-89356-593-5
            Hardcover   979-8-89356-592-8

Library of Congress Control Number: 2024903112

Contents

ACKNOWLEDGEMENTS

I am thankful to my two ex-wives, Mary and Kem (consecutive, of course, not concurrent), my brothers, Ted and Patrick, and my children for having taken the time to read my draft and providing me with such things as dates certain things happened, the correct weights and lengths of newborns, the spelling of grandchildren's names, and filling me in on details of incidents which they remembered, but I hadn't.

An additional, special "Thank You!" to Kem, who, even though we're divorced, has agreed to proof-read my manuscript. Her memory about things is much better than mine, and I've made the corrections and additions she has recommended. She'll always be Sparkle to me.

It's interesting to me how things they remembered helped to "jar" memories I had of other incidents, which I included after their review and assistance.

Above all, I thank my Lord for the talent He provided me to be able to put this all together.

PREFACE

I am writing this revised autobiography in my 76th year, inspired by my younger daughter, Laura, who suggested I put my life in writing for family and friends interested in knowing more about me. I've included things that have occurred during my lifetime – some happy, some sad, and some just happened.

I am a Christian, primarily, a part of the body of Jesus Christ, having first been baptized at the age of 10 at the Ashland Christian Church, which was Presbyterian. I had a second baptism at the age of 28 at the Worldwide Church of God, at the time a very legalistic church, full of God's love, just lacking grace. Since I left that church, it has since converted to Christ-centered worship, and has changed its name to Grace Communion International. I am now (May of 2022), and have been for a number of years, a member of the Mesa First Church of the Nazarene, in Mesa, Arizona, which has very recently (finally) gotten its name changed to Journey of Grace Church of the Nazarene. It was the first Nazarene church started here in 1959, but the Pastor, Church Board, and the majority of the congregation agreed that a more appropriate name would be Journey of Grace, as opposed to Mesa First. It more fittingly describes our present mission, since God's grace is much more important that being Mesa's "first" Nazarene church, as we are on a "Journey of Grace."

I gave this book the title, "THE PATHS OF MY LIFE" because I know God guided me on His path. There are times I followed the Holy Spirit's guidance, and other times I went and did what I pleased, justifying my actions one way or another. So, I was either on God's path for my life, or my own path, learning different lessons on each. Of course, I've learned God's path is clearly the better of the two. I am the person I am today because of the path I chose to follow at any particular time. I will also add here whichever path I may have been on, each and every event in my life had a purpose. It's important to note here that God's path for me has not always been the easier one, but has resulted in my being blessed by Him much more, because of my having followed His guidance.

The two main principles Mom and Dad drove into the minds of my siblings and myself were honesty and respecting other people and their property. I'll be the first to admit I've not been perfect in either, but my daily goal is to do both. Part of honesty is making and keeping commitments, which I give a very high priority daily. I am a very positive-minded person, and when others I'm talking with start complaining about people or situations, I do my best to bring up the positive characteristics of the person, or good things about the situation.

I've been married to two women (as stated in the acknowledgments, the marriages were consecutive, not concurrent). My first wife, Mary, left me because of "that weird religion" I was in, and also, as she stated, because I was very controlling. My second wife, Kem, and I were married the first time for almost 25 years. It was a second marriage for the both of us. Kem's first husband, David, left her because he didn't want Kem making obedience to God more important than what he wanted her to do. Then, after having been divorced for a bit over seven-and-a-half years, Kem and I remarried, only to end up divorced again after almost four years. I'll mention here that while Kem and I have no children of our own, she has been a most lovingly dedicated "step" Mother to Mary's and my children, grandchildren, and great-grandchildren. She has also graciously loved and accepted my entire family, as you'll see in the story.

I spent nine years in the military, and requested a Conscientious Objector discharge, because of my religious beliefs at that time. I was a Staff Sergeant when I was discharged from the Army. I must have been very convincing concerning my request for an early discharge. Even the Senior Chaplain of the Berlin Brigade, Colonel Rockwell, recommended approval of my request.

I guess that's enough preface. I don't want to put my entire life story here. It's only supposed to be a "pre-face" to the story. So, here goes . . . . .

CHAPTER ONE

My Very Early Years

As with most lives, mine started at birth (actually, it is my firm belief that life begins at conception). I was born about two months following the conclusion of World War II. That made me a "pre-boomer," since I was born so soon after the end of the war. My Dad had a severe right arm injury, which prevented his qualifying to enter the military. More on that later.

I came into the world in Mercy Hospital on the south side of Chicago. While a much more modern hospital is there now, the building in which I was born has since been torn down, and a multi-level parking garage has been erected to make it easier for doctors and patients to find a place to park. So the room where I was born was converted into a parking space.

These very early years must have been quite uneventful, as I only remember one incident when I was about four years old. The four of us kids (Ted, Ruth, Juanita, and me) must have gotten terribly dirty playing outside. There were four laundry wash tubs in the other part of the basement from the apartment in which we lived. Mom made all four of us take off all our dirty clothes as she filled all four tubs with water, and each of us got into one of the tubs, for Mom to scrub us clean. She got us clean clothes to put on as she finished with each of us. She never had to do that again!

My first memory (not at home) is of a wooden red truck that was my favorite toy in kindergarten.* When the class photo was taken, the teacher let me put the truck in front of me on the floor, to include it in the picture. While it wasn't mine to keep, I really enjoyed playing with it.

I do remember one time playing with matches, and Mom caught me. She made me light a match and hold it until I felt the heat from the flame. I never again played with matches!

I have one older brother, Ted, and two older sisters, Ruth and Juanita. My younger brother Patrick was born shortly before we moved. We had to move, 'cause with the new baby, the apartment was just much too small. We lived in a three-room basement flat. The front room was Mom and Dad's bedroom, and the one bedroom slept us four kids, with two sets of bunk beds; the girls on one side of the room, and Ted and me on the other side.

Our apartment was kitty-corner from the Ashland Christian Church. We kids attended church most every Sunday. We first went to Sunday School classes, and then we'd go to the service and hear the minister talk. Pastor Traverse Harrison was our minister, a very nice person as best as I can remember. One Sunday, I had gotten a prize for Bible verse memorization. After church that day, some other kids and I were getting into mischief in part of the church we shouldn't have been in. When we heard an adult calling us to see what we were doing, we all ran. I tripped on something, and the 'prize' I had broke into a myriad of pieces, cutting open my left hand at the base of my index finger in the process. I ended up getting stitches. It healed up okay, but left a scar that I have to this day. We also occasionally attended Bible Study on Wednesday nights, at a Baptist church a few blocks away from home, called Gospel Hall.

Pigeons in our church bell tower were a big problem, and Dad was hired by the church to go up in the tower and kill them. He'd just get hold of them, twist their neck (which killed them instantly), and then throw them down 'til he had a bunch of them. He then put them in plastic bags and threw them out in the trash.

The church had a very exquisite pipe organ, and the organist really made it 'sing!' The pipes were located high up on the wall on either side of the stage. I enjoyed singing in the children's choir, as well as singing the hymns with the congregation during services. I was baptized when I was ten years old. The hymn that was playing when I went forward to confess my sins and accept Jesus as my Savior, was "Oh, How I Love Jesus." It was on page 262 of the hymnal. (I like, and remember, many different numbers throughout my life.) Two children in my Sunday School class were my best friend, Don Romanosky, and my cousin, Bill Smith.

*Kindergarten is a German word, meaning "children's garden."

CHAPTER TWO

My Parents and Siblings

I think it significant to mention here that I only really knew one of my grandparents, my Dad's Mom, Clara Cora Dornan. I lived at Grandma's house for about one year of my time in high school. Grandpa, John Frost Dornan, died when I was only five years old, and Grandma never remarried. All I remember about him was that he had a very deep voice, he was really tall, and he was a deacon in our church. I wasn't allowed to go to the funeral, because I was told I was too young. My Mom's Dad (Martin Darst) died when she was a little girl, and then her Mom married Charlie Fox. In my lifetime, I think we visited Grandma Fox maybe three or four times, and I think she came to visit us twice. She and Grandpa Fox lived in Warsaw, Ohio, and because we didn't travel much as a family, we just didn't get to see them very often.

The reason I mention this is because, here I am, 76 years old, with three children, nine grandchildren, and about 14 great-grandchildren (I've lost count). In my earlier autobio, I included seven great-grandchildren when Sharlene (Marty Jr's daughter) married a gentleman with seven children. One of Timm's older daughters had a child, so that would have been one great-great grandchild. A few years ago, I was invited to, and went to, Shar and Timm's wedding in Aurora, Illinois, in which I proudly walked her down the aisle. But unfortunately, after having a child of their own, their marriage turned sour, and they divorced, but on good terms. Since they divorced, I took "Timm's" seven children off our family tree, and added the one that Shar and Timm had between them. I get to occasionally see a few of my grandchildren who live in the Phoenix Valley, Elizabeth, Jerry, and Kathryn. Sharlene, Katlin, Jessica, and Joey live in Illinois. We (the family in general) haven't heard from Micheal since the day after he got out of prison in January, 2020. I pray he's in good health and will someday contact us. And Alex joined the Navy and is a crew member on the U.S.S. Toledo, a nuclear submarine, as their radio operator. We're all very proud of him.

Just being able to communicate with them is a real thrill for me. I just hope I can be a positive influence on their lives. A goal I have is to see them all more often, just to share time with them, and love them like my Grandma Dornan loved me.

Grandma Dornan was a prim and proper lady. She dressed very pretty, and wore the most decorative hats to church. One time when I was having dinner at Grandma's house, she asked me to put new butter in the butter dish. She was very proud of me for unwrapping the butter and putting it in the dish without once having touched the butter. She said, "Thank you! That's the proper way to do it!" My older brother, Ted, said that we were taught how to properly unwrap butter by TV cowboy Bob Archer. I don't remember that cowboy, but Ted reminded me of that. Sometimes, Grandma would fall asleep watching television, but when told she was sleeping, she responded with, "I was only resting my eyelids!" Uncle Ray would then tell her, "But you were snoring!" She would immediately retort with, **"I don't snore!"** She was really a very pleasant lady to be around. When Grandma was younger, she was a professional opera singer, but as she got older, her singing voice just wasn't what it used to be, but at church, she still sang the hymns out in praise to our Lord. It reminds me that God says in the Bible to, "make a joyful noise." He doesn't say to sing perfectly. He loves us in spite of our imperfections. Grandma didn't worry about who didn't like her singing voice, 'cause she knew God liked it!

My Dad, Kenneth Joseph Dornan, born August 15, 1916, worked for most of his life as a machinist, dealing in very miniscule measurements, cutting keyways in gears, as well as many other types of machining. The cutting had to be very accurate, most times within one to two thousandths of an inch! Dad was very proud of the work he did.

When he was only twenty years old, he was turning the crank on the front of a Mack truck (this was in 1936) to get it started. The crank kicked back, flew out of his grip, and smashed his right arm at the wrist. Dad's wrist bone was shattered so severely that a bone had to be grafted from his right leg to replace it. While he did lose the use of his right wrist, not being able to turn it at all, he was still able to use his right hand, once the arm healed. This injury prevented him from going into the military. It was during the six months that his right arm was in a cast that he became ambidextrous (able to write with either hand).

Many days, on the way home from work, he would stop at a tavern near the shop, have a beer, and put a bet down on the horses. He didn't win very often. I know that, 'cause when he did, he'd buy us all something special, usually an expensive cut of beef that he'd prepare when he got home. That was a real treat, since Mom normally didn't get enough grocery money to get things like that.

Along with honesty and respecting other people's property, which both Mom and Dad taught us, Dad also taught me to *never* hit a woman. That's why Dad left Mom and us kids. One evening when Mom and Dad were arguing, Mom slapped him across the face, scratching him with her nails. Rather than strike back, he just left the house. I just ran into my room, crawled under my bed, and cried myself to sleep.

After he left, I understand Dad gave Mom (if I remember right) his entire net pay from Industrial Gear. He would supplement his income by working a few nights a week at the Block Brothers' service station, driving a tow truck.

Occasionally, he would invite me to go with him on the tow truck, when there wasn't school the next day. It was really exciting to go on the tow truck, mostly because I was just able to spend time with him. He'd send me to the store a short block from the station to get a quart of Canfield's pop and a package of Twinkies, which we'd share. That was a very special treat for me! He'd give me a $20 bill, and then put the change in the register, so, if needed, he'd have change for customers who might come in to buy gas. One time it was very snowy when I went to buy the soda and Twinkies, and I lost the $20 bill before I got to the store. Thankfully, I did find it when I went back to look for it in the snow, and then bought the snacks for Dad to share with me.

When Dad left home, he went to live with Grandma Dornan, and slept in a room in the attic of her bungalow. One time when he said he was coming to visit us kids, I grew impatient. Grandma's house was less than two miles away, so I decided to walk over there to see Dad, and get a ride back home. Well, he had already left when I got there, so I ran as fast as I could back home. He didn't visit very long, and was gone by the time I got back. Even though

I knew it was my own fault, I ran into my bedroom and cried, disappointed at not seeing him.

One thing Dad taught me, inadvertently, was to use friendly nicknames for women in my life. I'm not just sure why, but he would call Mom nicknames like "Battle-axe," "Toots," (rhymes with puts), or "the old lady." I clearly couldn't say anything about it, since I was only a kid, but I surely didn't like it. I set it in my mind that when I had a girlfriend or a wife that I would call her nice nicknames, and not ones like Dad used. Of course, I loved Dad, in spite of things I may not have liked about him. He actually taught me a lot about mechanics when I went with him on the tow truck, as well as when he was working on his car, and I could watch. Nowadays, with all the electronics that are put into cars that I've owned, I don't even change my own oil. Before all the electronics, I've replaced brakes, rebuilt carburetors, put new shocks on, among other things, but no more.

Some time after Dad and Mom separated, he found a lady friend named Lenore. He most likely knew her before his and Mom's separation, since she was a sister to Aunt Bernice (Dad's sister-in-law). They eventually were able to get a place of their own, and Dad moved out of Grandma Dornan's. Lenore was a nice lady for him, and I "kind of" was happy for Dad, but for the longest time, and even well into my adult years, I referred to Lenore as, "that woman," because I felt that she had taken Dad away from Mom. Once I got over the hatred (with God's help), I was able to talk to them about it, and I found out that wasn't true. It was just in my mind that Lenore (whom I called Norrie, once I became friendlier toward her), was preventing my parents from getting back together. That also wasn't true. My parents had no intentions of getting back together, whether or not Norrie was there.

Anyway, there were many happy memories with Dad and Norrie. One I recall was when I was my normal self, and throwing around my dry humor with "one-liners." I guess Norrie was getting tired of them (which didn't surprise me, as I can overdo it sometimes), and Norrie got her words mixed up. Instead of saying, "Where do you think you are?" she came out with, "Where you are?" Everyone started laughing, 'cause that was funnier than my "one-liners." Norrie even laughed, after she (almost immediately) realized what she had said. But I did take the hint, and laid low for a while, at least with my dry humor.

Dad had retired, and he and Norrie moved down to Robinson, Illinois. When he was in his mid-sixties, he was rushed to the Robinson hospital. It turned out that he had gone into a diabetic coma. Before that happened, he wasn't even aware that he was diabetic. After seven weeks, he was able to come home, and he had his insulin, needles, and other diabetic paraphernalia. I once asked him, "How can you stand giving yourself the shots?" He simply replied, "It's easy! I do it in my arm, my stomach, or my thigh." He was really good at it!

After a couple years of giving himself his shots, he just got tired of it, and Kem took over giving him his shots, and being his caregiver, until he went into the nursing home. Kem, being a CNA, (Certified Nurse's Assistant), was well qualified to care for him. While Dad lived with us, he had his own three-room apartment in our house, on the first floor. We lived upstairs. It was a 2-1/2 story bungalow with a full basement. Once when I was visiting with Dad in the dining room of the nursing home, he wanted to know how his room was. He was referring to his room at our house, and I knew that! But I told him, "Your room is fine! It's right down the hall here." I can't put his reply here. But then I hugged him, and told him that I loved him. I knew he wanted to go back home, and he just knew he wasn't going to, and he found it hard to accept. Dad ended up going to the hospital a number of times during his (six-month) stay in the nursing home, because he kept pulling out his IV (Intravenous) needle, and he had to go to the hospital to get it reinserted. The last time he went to the hospital, his heart started acting up, so the doctor decided it would be best to admit Dad. He lasted two weeks in the hospital. During one visit, he asked me to cut his fingernails, just 'cause I was the one who always did it, even though Kem was his caregiver while he was home. Well, I cut his nails, but trimmed one a bit close, and it started bleeding. I asked Kem to ask the nurse for a bandage. When she brought it, I put it on Dad's finger, kissed his finger, and told him, "There! Now it's all better!" He got the biggest smile on his face when I said that. A few days later, about 11:00 p.m., we got a call from the hospital that Dad was serious. When I got there, his doctor met me in the visitor's lounge, and let me know that in the last half hour, they had tried seven times to revive Dad, but to no avail. I told him just to let Dad go. He died that evening at the age of 75. A part of my heart went with him.

My Mom, Elsie Ruth (Darst) Dornan, born June 14, 1921, was a most patient person, and very loving. Many times, (when I was younger, of course), I would drive Mom to her wits end with my whining. She was a "stay-at-home" Mom, back when it was more common for the Mom to be at home, and the Dad would bring home the money to run the household. Before Dad left us, I believe it was difficulties with finances that caused the majority of their arguing. He didn't always give Mom the amount of money she felt she needed to properly feed and clothe us kids. Once he left, however, he voluntarily gave Mom most of his pay, and kept very little for himself.

Because of our tight financial situation, Mom learned how to become a "do-it-yourselfer" type of person. I remember one time she fixed up a scooter for me, and was bringing it into our apartment to hide in her closet, to surprise me with it, but I saw her bringing it in. It was a time of mixed emotions for me, because I knew she wanted to surprise me. Now it wouldn't be a surprise. I was sad that I saw her with the scooter, but I was also very excited to know that I would have one for my very own! And I didn't even worry that it wasn't "brand new." I was just thrilled to have it.

A couple years after Dad left, Mom got a friend named Ralph. He was a lot of fun to be around, except when he was drinking. I remember one time when Ralph and I were playing penny-ante poker. He won all the pennies I had, and I whined, "You're not going to take all my pennies, are you?" He gave me back my pennies, but at the same time, he told me something I never forgot, to this day. He said, "If you can't afford to lose, you shouldn't gamble." The memory of that saying is always in my mind, and I can always think of a better way to spend my money than to waste it away on gambling. Mom tried time after time to get him to at least slow down his alcoholic intake, but he just kept it up. Finally, she just told him to stop coming around. After a few times of pleading to keep seeing her, he quit coming around. A couple years later, Ralph's Mom died, which left Ralph very emotionally distressed. Shortly after his Mom died, Ralph committed suicide.

I believe that was after Mom met and fell in love with an especially nice man named Nestor. They spent a lot of time together, and Mom was really happy with him. It turned out that Nestor was married. And this is the weird part (at least to me) . . . Mom and Nestor's wife turned out to be really good friends! Mom saw him for many years, and then he found out he had cancer. He only lasted a short time after that. He was in his hospital room, in a lot of pain (in spite of the medications he was being given to alleviate the pain), when Mom told him, "It's okay to let go, honey." He died that same night.

Nestor's widow invited Mom to his funeral, and they remained friends for many years afterwards.

My sister Ruth was still living at home with Mom, so at least Mom had someone with her. After Nestor died, Mom never even looked for another man. Mom was renting a very inexpensive apartment on the south side of Chicago, at West 47th Street and South Racine Avenue. She was 70 years old when Dad died, in early January, 1992. Up until that time, she was living on a very small Social Security check, along with the help that Ruth provided. I informed Mom that she could increase her check by drawing on Dad's Social Security. She had no idea she could do that. It increased her check substantially. She was really excited about the increased amount of her check. She then got involved with other seniors, and travelled all over the United States, mostly on bus tours to different states.

Ruth died of a stroke that December, the same year Dad died. It was shortly after Thanksgiving weekend. It was Ruth's second stroke that killed her. Her first stroke was in July, 1992, which left her needing constant nursing care. I remember one time going to visit her. The nurse would put Ruth in a wheel chair to sit up, so she wouldn't be in bed all day. Because of the stroke, Ruth wasn't able to talk, but she could still have fun. While she was sitting in the wheel chair, she would wriggle her hips until she would slide (gently) out of the wheel chair and land on the floor. Then she would sit there and laugh. I got the biggest kick out of that. I was very glad she could find a reason to laugh, because I know she was very frustrated, cooped up in that room, and unable to get "out and about," as she was so used to doing. She was very active in her church, and the stroke caused a major life change for her. And then the second stroke, as the doctor described to me, just "fried her brain," and she passed away. Mom was on her own after that.

When Mom was about 74, her cardiologist put her in the hospital for quadruple bypass surgery, which turned into a quintuple bypass. She came through feeling great! Kem and I had offered to take care of her if she'd move down to Arizona to be with us. For a couple years, she kept refusing, being as independent as she could. So, we quit asking her, and started praying about it. Then, about two years later, she called us, and asked if there were a nursing home she could stay at in Arizona. I told her, "No, but you can come live with us." At about 80 years old, she came to live with Kem and me.

After Mom moved in with us, she asked us to fly up to Chicago to drive her car down to Arizona. I had something medical going on at the time, so I was unable to make the trip. Kem agreed to go alone, so she flew up to Chicago. She got to Mom's place okay, and loaded up her yellow car (we don't remember the make) with a number of boxes that Mom wanted. They filled up the back seat. Kem was on her way when, in St. Joseph, Missouri, the car died. The mechanic told her it was beyond repair. The repair shop there offered to buy the car, which worked out okay, but Kem and the boxes still needed to get to Arizona. Kem was able to get a ticket on the Greyhound bus, and paid extra to take all the boxes on the same bus. It was quite frustrating and discouraging, but Kem managed to get everything done that was needed, and completed her trip back to Arizona on the bus.

Not long after that, to get her furniture down to Arizona, Kem and I flew to Chicago, and then rented a Budget truck. The trip was mostly uneventful, except for two things that happened along the way, one negative and one positive. The worst part of our trip was driving on the interstate in Arkansas. The right lane of the interstate was in dire need of repair. We literally bounced in our seats the entire time we remained in the right lane. I would ride the left lane as much as possible, but then move into the right lane when another vehicle wanted to pass. Except for that, the trip went fine. Something I didn't think about at the time, but is quite possible, is that the Budget truck needed new shock absorbers. That just might have alleviated, or at least lessened, the bouncing we experienced.

At one truck stop in Texas, we saw a couple driving a semi. They had a Bengal tiger cub as their traveling companion. They had gotten permission from the authorities to have it with them. It was still quite tame, and very playful. Its paws were the size of my fists! The couple understood that once it reached a certain age, they'd need to turn it over to a zoo, but they were thoroughly enjoying it in the meantime. That was a most pleasant experience!

Mom stayed with us about eighteen months, and then requested to move with Ted and Faye (my brother and sister-in-law) in Aurora, Colorado. She was with them for a few months, but then circumstances required Mom to move into assisted living. That went okay for a year or so, but then Mom started deteriorating. She went into a nursing home, and then to a facility for hospice. All through this, Mom kept her wits about her, but we could see her fading away. One thing I remember during the time she was in assisted living, she had her own room, but it wasn't locked. Anytime Mom couldn't find something, she said someone stole it. But then when she found it, she would say, "Oh! They brought it back!" We just got a kick out of that. Ted and I both have a very dry humor, and even up to the last, Mom would still laugh at our jokes. Mom died at 83, after having lived a very full life.

My siblings are (in order of age) Ted (Theodore Allen Dornan), Ruth Elaine Dornan, Juanita Irene (Dornan-Thomas-Derrington) Davis, and my younger brother Patrick Kenneth Dornan. Each has their own special-ness in my life.

Of my four siblings, Ted (born February 18, 1940) had the greatest influence on my life. He had been in the Army, so I decided to do the same. He joined the Worldwide Church of God when I was 18 or so, which I joined nine years later. I'm getting a bit ahead of myself, (which is actually quite difficult to do, since I am where I am), so I'll back up a little.

In my growing up years, I remember wrestling with Ted, and having lots of fun with my big brother. There were times, however, that we had problems. One thing that happened, I'll explain just by quoting Ted . . . "After coming home from church, and hearing those little old ladies keep repeating how I was such a nice boy, I'd come home and beat up on you (meaning yours truly), until you started crying, just to show I wasn't such a nice boy as they would claim." There were also times I deserved it, though, because I was a terrible tease. There were times I'd torment Ted until he'd start beating on me, just to get me to stop. Then, when he did that, I'd start laughing (I'm not sure why), so he'd retaliate by hitting me until I started crying. Then he'd leave me alone.

I really missed him when he went off to college. He went to Manhattan Bible College in Manhattan, Kansas, to become a minister. That never came to fruition, since he was introduced to the Radio Church of God (which became the Worldwide Church of God), and that church did not follow traditional Christian practices. To describe the practices for people today to understand them, I would say they were more Jewish than Christian. While that church did recognize Jesus as God, it did not recognize the grace that Jesus provides us through His sacrifice and death on the cross. It was a very legalistic church. It was required to observe the Sabbath, from sundown Friday to sundown Saturday. There were annual Holy Days which were mandatory to observe, unless one was truly physically unable to do so, and we were permitted to eat only the 'clean' foods as described in the Old Testament. We could not eat shellfish, nor could we eat pork, rabbit, or other animals which did not have cloven hooves and chewed the cud. The reasoning behind this (which is actually quite valid) is the food eaten does not go through the same digestive process as that of the clean animals, and the meat these animals produce is not healthy for human consumption.

Another reason is because most unclean animals are scavengers, and they can eat and digest many substances which *they* can tolerate, but which cause sickness in humans. These substances end up in the cuts of meat in the grocery store and on our plates. To this day, the only unclean meat I do eat is the pepperoni or small sausage pieces on pizza, and a rare slice of ham.

Anyway, back to Ted. He went into the Army (I believe it was the Reserve), and spent some time at Fort Leonard Wood, Missouri, which he called, "Fort Lost-in-the-Woods." He met and married Joanne Chapman, from Findlay, Ohio, on April 21, 1974. She was divorced, and had four children; Sheryl, Freidia, Billy Joe, and Aaron. They then had twin boys, to add to the family he married into. They were Timothy and Jeffrey, born a couple years after they got married. The boys were premature, and spent some time in the Pediatric Intensive Care Unit, since they were both well under five pounds. Ted and Joanne took them home, still a bit under the five-pound desired weight, but their doctor agreed to it, and the boys were fine and healthy. Joanne developed cancer, and refused the radiation treatment for two reasons. The first reason she gave was she didn't want the horrendous side effects of the treatment, and secondly, because she would have had to have traveled from Beatrice, Nebraska to Omaha, for the treatments, which would have been an 80-mile round trip. That lengthy ride, combined with the pain she was in, she said probably would have killed her sooner than the cancer itself. She died of cancer at home on December 3, 1989.

A few years later, Ted met Faye James, who had also lost her spouse to cancer. They counseled with their minister, and when they got married, I was their best man. Kem, my sister Juanita, and I were all able to make the trip from Arizona to Colorado for Ted and Faye's wedding. Just from my personal observation, theirs was a match made in heaven. They complemented, supported, and encouraged each other, and when needed, gave gentle correction to each other. Unfortunately, after about seventeen years, it ended up in divorce.

Ted got involved with a religious group from Florida, which Faye didn't approve of, because of certain beliefs. It wound up that Ted moved to Florida, with Faye refusing to accompany him. She divorced him, and a couple years later, he married Linda Claire Lopez, and she became Linda Claire (Lopez) Dornan. I've not gotten to meet her, but we have talked on the phone, and she seems to be quite a lovely lady, and a true blessing for Ted.

My sister, Ruth, born November 4, 1941, lived with Mom her entire life. The best I can tell, she never had any interest in marriage. I don't remember teasing her as much as I did Ted or Juanita. She's the quieter of my two sisters, who stayed more to herself. Ruth had Rheumatic Fever when she was very young, which resulted in her need of a mitral valve replacement in her heart. As well as living with Mom her whole life, Ruth was also deeply involved in her church. When she was in her early 40's, I helped her learn how to drive. Mom's friend, Nestor, also helped her in learning her driving "experience." She did quite well, but right around 50 years old, due to her heart condition, she had to quit driving. Actually, Mom was quite pleased when Ruth had to quit driving. There was one church member who took full advantage of Ruth driving her virtually everywhere she needed to go, and that upset Mom. The day before she had her first stroke in July, 1992, I was blessed to have seen her on my way to work. We talked for a couple minutes, and the last words she said to me were, "You'd better go catch your bus, so you're not late for work." That was the last time I heard her speak intelligible words. The next day at work, another employee found Ruth on the floor of the restroom. She was rushed to the hospital, where it was confirmed she had a stroke. It affected her left side, and she wasn't able to speak, but she was able to show emotions. When we'd come to visit, she would actually have fun. The staff would sit her in a wheel chair next to her bed, and she would wriggle her hips until she slid out of the chair onto the floor. Then she'd just sit there and laugh, sort of saying, "Ha! Ha! I did it again!!" Also, Mom could make her laugh, by whispering, "Oh, Shit!" in her ear. We're not certain why that made her laugh. Mom found that out by accident. It might have been 'cause Ruth (to the best of my knowledge) never uttered a cuss word in her entire life, and when Mom cussed, it struck her funny bone. Sometimes she would cry, and I'm certain that was because she couldn't express herself in words. Ruth had a second, more severe, stroke shortly after Thanksgiving, in early December of 1992, which caused her death. The doctor said, "It just fried her brain!" I know she's much happier now! Ruth's life was a life of service to her church, as well as helping Mom as much as she could. She just enjoyed helping friends in general. At Ruth's wake, the chairs were all filled in the room where she was laid out, and the funeral parlor set up extra chairs in the hall outside her room. When her minister spoke, he told the overflow crowd (which included many of Ruth's church friends) that Ruth set a most loving example of service, and that others would do well to follow her example. She clearly left a legacy!

Juanita, the younger of my two older sisters, was born on July 17, 1943. I was closer to Juanita than I was to Ruth. It's not that I loved her more, it's just we had more camaraderie, and spent more time together. I tormented and teased her much more than I ever should have, now that I look back on it. We lived in a basement apartment (with tile covering a concrete floor), and one Christmas, Juanita got a doll with a head that rattled. Well, I wanted to see what made the head rattle, so I grabbed the doll by the feet, and smashed its head on the floor. I promptly found out what made the head rattle. Pieces of the hard, plastic head went all over, along with the pebbles and the eyes. I felt really bad after I did it. I don't remember the punishment I got.

Another time when I was tormenting her, she picked up a Melmac (supposedly unbreakable plastic) plate, and threw it at me. I ducked. It hit the wall behind me, and broke into what seemed to be a million pieces. Juanita cried because the plate broke, and I cried because she cried. I was really quite a tease when I was younger. I thankfully grew out of it.

Juanita had trouble finding a kind, loving husband. Her first marriage was to a man (Michael), whose morals left a lot to be desired. She divorced him after a very short marriage. Bill, her second husband, lasted longer, but he abused her physically and verbally, and she finally divorced him. Then she met Darrell. I would describe him as her "Prince Charming!" They lived together, but never got married. However, they lived together long enough to be common-law husband and wife. And he was the best thing that happened to Juanita. He was kind, loving, patient, had a great sense of humor, and was just overall good to her. Juanita developed a very serious case of Rheumatoid Arthritis, and could hardly walk. Darrell's nickname for her was, "Flash!" He did it good-naturedly, and she took it the same way. Sometimes, when he'd ask her to do something, she'd wait a few seconds, and then say, "Do you want to see me do it again?" Then they'd laugh till their sides would hurt. Unfortunately, he died very young of a heart attack. Juanita lived in a small town in Kentucky, and since there was no one else she was very close to there, she called Kem and me, and asked if she could come live with us. Of course, we said, "Yes!" When I told her there's just one thing I'd need from her, she said, "I know. I'll quit smoking when I come there." And she did. She had about half a pack of cigarettes when she got here. She smoked them out on the front porch, and then quit . . . **cold turkey!** About a year after she quit, she bummed a cigarette from a neighbor, lit it, and didn't even finish it. She didn't even like it! And she never had another one.

Kem became her caregiver, as she had been for Dad up in Chicago. The only difference was, here in Arizona, the State pays a qualified caregiver, even if the caregiver is a relative! Since Kem was a Certified Nurse's Assistant, she got paid for taking care of Juanita. While Juanita lived with us, she got both knees replaced (one at a time, of course), and went from a wheel chair, to a walker, to a cane, and then to just her two legs. After that, the only time we'd put her in a wheel chair was if we went to a grocery store or a large department store where there would be a lot of walking, 'cause excessive walking would still wear Juanita down. But, other than that, she did just fine! When Juanita came to live with us, we found her to be most easy-going and laid back. We got along quite well, and Mom was really pleased, since she remembered how I was when we were younger.

Juanita was on quite a number of medications because of her infirmities, and they severely weakened her body's immune system. One Sunday afternoon, while we were living in Tucson, she was coughing up blood, so Kem took her to the emergency room. She was admitted, and *called* us that evening on the phone. She talked with Kem first, and then with me. The only words I remember from her were, "Marty, I feel terrible!" and that was in a very weak voice. Then she had to hang up, because the doctor had just come into the room. That same night, she ended up in the Intensive Care Unit. The next morning, about 9:00 a.m., we got a call from the hospital that she had died. The diagnosis was double pneumonia and a weak heart. She lived the last three years of her life with us, and I'm grateful to God for that opportunity. She'll always hold a soft spot in my heart.

My younger brother, Patrick Kenneth Dornan, was born on February 25, 1956, just four days away from being a "leap year" baby. I was ten years old when he was born, and was both big brother and father to him. Dad and Mom separated when he was about eighteen months old. I believe Ted had already moved out, and I just don't remember Ruth or Juanita taking care of him very much. They very well may have, but I just don't remember. Except for caring for him when he was young, I wasn't very close to Patrick. Circumstances just happened that way. I really missed Dad when he moved out, and went to see him as much as I could. For whatever reasons, at that time in my life, seeing Dad had a higher priority than helping with Patrick. Then Mom let me move out to live with Dad at Grandma Dornan's, and I rarely saw Patrick after that. I still love him, of course, and, at that time, we'd talk occasionally, but were just not very close. I do remember Mom and us kids going to Rainbow Beach (near 75th Street and Lake Michigan), when Patrick was about two years old. He had recently been potty trained. When he went into the water, he came back carrying his swimming trunks, because they were wet. Mom, of course, put them right back on him. He said, "But Mommy, they're wet!!" Mom promptly explained that at the beach it's okay for your swimsuit to get wet. Then he understood, and went back into the water, and left them on.

From 2005 until late 2007, Patrick roomed with Mary (Mother of our children) and her friend Evan. They helped him to get out of a really bad situation (drugs, alcohol, etc.), helping him to clean up his act. He went to work regularly, saved up some money, and to the best of my knowledge, he's been avoiding the stuff that messed up his mind. My prayer then, and even now, is that God will help him stay on the right track, so he can continue to make something out of his life. From living with Mary and Evan, he moved to his own place on West 47th Street and South Ashland Avenue. He still worked for the same security firm he worked for when he roomed with Mary and Evan. I believe the help they gave Patrick was worthwhile. I do know that when he left their place, he didn't tell them anything. He just left and went on his own. I believe he left, because he got tired of being told what to do, and how to run his life. I talked with him on the phone, and he didn't sound drugged up, so that was a real blessing. He also was attending a Christian church weekly, and I praise our Lord for that!

Thanksgiving of 2009 found Patrick living in Lyons, Illinois, a suburb of Chicago. He was still attending church and staying away from illegal drugs. I talked with him and let him know how proud I was of him.

That was the last I heard from him for almost twelve years. I've done internet searches, getting residence addresses he's had and mailing letters to each of the addresses I could find. I asked him to either respond to me or contact family there in Illinois, so we could know he was still alive. Mary had also, using local contacts, tried locating him, without success. Then finally, late in 2020, because he had gotten his own apartment, an internet search picked up his address, phone number, etc., and I was able to call him, and talk with him. He was quite surprised to hear from me. He told me he was under the impression that his family had basically disowned him. I let him know that was far from the truth, and that all these years, I had repeatedly attempted to find out his whereabouts, unsuccessfully, until this latest internet search. We talked for quite a while. I was just so happy to hear his voice. I called other family members, and gave his phone number to them, asking them to call him. Some did, and some didn't want to bother. I got permission from some of them to give Patrick their number, so he could call them directly, to try and re-establish a relationship with him, to help him feel more like family than an outcast. I had to really convince him to call Evan, since the two of them didn't get along well, mostly due to Patrick being high on whatever, and Evan letting him know he had to get off that "stuff." He ended up listening to Evan and Mary, but never had gotten over his upset with Evan, until I convinced him to call Evan and apologize for his behavior. He did that, and surprised Evan and Mary when he apologized. Their relationship still needs work, but at least that much was accomplished.

CHAPTER THREE

My School Remembrances

As I mentioned earlier, I remember my red wooden truck from kindergarten. Through grammar school, I generally did well with my grades. In first grade, the art teacher would only work with those students who showed some signs of doing well. At least, that was my impression. I didn't do well at all, and consequently got very little help with learning how to improve my artwork. To this day, I don't do well with freehand art, and have no desire to do so. I attribute it to my first-grade art experience. However, while I try not to blame the teacher, I do feel if she would have been more patient with me, I might have progressed much better in this area. I also believe if I had been more self-motivated, I could have practiced more and done better. While I never took mechanical drawing in school, I have found that I do like this type of art, making different designs with drawing tools.

Mom raised us kids on Scrabble, and I think that really helped me in school. I've always done well in English class, including reading, writing compositions, and with grammar and punctuation. My kids can attest to the "grammar" part in conversations where they are talking about themselves and one other person. They might say, "Me and Johnny walked to school together." They would say it fast enough that it sounded like "Mean Johnny," and I would say, "I didn't know Johnny was mean!" That was only to emphasize that when we are talking (or writing) about another person (or persons) and ourselves, it's always proper English to put ourselves last (i.e., Johnny and I walked to school together.) They would then "correct" what they said, after a "Yes, Dad!" I would usually end up in the spelling bees, and do quite well. I never made it to the top, but the one spelling bee I remember being dropped out of was because of misspelling the word, "separate." I spelled it, "seperate." I went to Earle School in Chicago for kindergarten through 5th grade. Then we moved out of our three-room basement apartment, to a three bedroom flat at 7348 South Green Street, in another school district. I then went to Oglesby School for 6th and 7th grades. It was while we lived on Green Street that Juanita graduated from grammar school. She then went to Calumet High School, and, even though we moved out of Calumet's district while she was attending there, she was able to continue going there through to graduation. I mention that, because Mom liked the old neighborhood better, so we moved back into Earle's district, where I completed 8th grade, and graduated.

I've also composed much poetry, starting in my teen years. I generally write poems as God inspires me. I've written concerning friendships, nature, my relationship with, and faith in God, and many other subjects. I've even occasionally written poems for my friends who wanted to impress their girlfriend. They would tell me about her, and I would put it into poetry and give it to them for her. I never kept those poems personally. It was just for the two of them. I enjoy doing things like that! I thank God for my poetic talent. I published my poetry in early 2013, in a book entitled, "Poetry in Emotion – a Christian's Perspective," by a self-publisher, "xlibris.com."

Ted, Ruth, and I all went to Lindblom High School. Patrick, if I remember right, attended Harper High School, the same high school our Dad attended. Dad actually attended Harper High, when it was converted from a middle school to a high school, so he attended Harper for six years. My grammar school years were overall uneventful. I remember a number of times that my parents didn't have enough funds for clothing or shoes, and (someone at) Earle School would provide me with new shoes, and a couple pairs of slacks and shirts. One time, I had just gotten a new pair of gym shoes. I was walking home from school. I was across the alley from Fire House #64, which was on the same street as our apartment. I saw a broken coke bottle, and in my mind, I thought, "I wonder what would happen if I stepped on that?" My mind went blank, and the next thing I knew, I was sitting in front of the fire house, crying, and a fireman had taken my shoe and sock off and wrapped a bunch of gauze around it, rather tight, to help stop the bleeding in my right foot. Someone went and got my Mom. She took me to the hospital. I don't remember how I got there, but I ended up getting twelve stitches in my foot. I actually felt worse about the brand-new shoes that I ruined than I did about my injured foot. I believe I was about eight years old when that happened. I graduated from Earle School third in rank out of 36 students. Some of the other students gave me the nickname, "The Brain." I didn't mind it, and I tried not to let it go "to my head!" (tee-hee). The two students that ranked higher than me were Leonard Bellanger and Kathleen Hanrahan. I really liked Kathy a lot, but was too shy to say anything.

While in 8th grade, we had a dance class which was canceled very shortly after it started. This was in the 1958-59 school year, and our school was just starting to be integrated. The two black students in our class were Cleo Brown and Leroy Washington. They were both quite personable, very friendly, and very good friends of mine. My parents taught us to like all people, regardless of their race or culture. Anyway, the dance class was canceled, because some prejudiced students refused to dance with Cleo or Leroy, simply because they were black. I was extremely disappointed when that happened. I understood why, but just didn't like it *at all*!

While I was quite the outgoing personality in grammar school, in high school I became quite introverted. During the first three years, I would stay to myself, and was absent much more than I really should have been. I would make up excuses, and I would just keep after Mom, until she would get very frustrated, sick of hearing my whining, and let me stay home. (A short note here) Because I saw what my whining did to Mom, I forbade my children from whining, to me or their Mom. Anytime they started whining, I would say, "I don't hear you." They started to whine louder, which I stopped immediately, and told them to ask what they wanted without whining, and I might allow them to do what they were asking. That's how they learned not to whine, and I was very grateful they learned that! Because of my excessive absences the first three years, it took me 4-1/2 years to complete high school, and that included going to summer school every year. The multitude of absences caused me to fail many classes. I had the ability, but not the right attitude. That changed my senior year.

I really "buckled down" that last year, and made top grades, which qualified me for the Honor Society. My overall grade point average (GPA) when I graduated, was 1.997, out of a possible 4.000. I ended up graduating in the top 10% of the bottom half of my class, nothing to be proud of. Because of those first three years, my GPA really suffered, due to my overall attitude and excessive absences.

I did participate in the R.O.T.C. (Reserve Officer's Training Corps) while attending Lindblom. I felt privileged to have graduated the same year that our R.O.T.C. class was ranked first out of all 32 high schools in Chicago. I enjoyed that class, I think mainly because I made it up to the rank of Captain, and I was a Company Commander. It helped me feel better about myself.

I also got involved in the (Lindblom Leader) school newspaper, the Bookkeeping Club, selling the (Eagle) school yearbook, and other extracurricular activities. I was the only male student in Office Practice, as well as Typing, because they all go hand-in-hand. I enjoyed all the attention I got in these classes, as the only guy. But I still was too self-conscious to ask to see any girls after school. Typing took a lot of patience, since there were numerous repetitive practices. But I'm extremely pleased I took it, since the keyboard for typewriters is generally the same layout used for computers, and I'm using that talent to prepare the manuscripts for both my books.

Thirteen years after graduating from Lindblom, since I was between jobs at the time, I took advantage of my veteran's benefits, which paid for my tuition at Richard J. Daley Community College, and gave me sufficient funds to cover my basic expenses while attending school. The college was located near the Ford City Shopping Center on the south side of Chicago. I utilized my abilities from the start at Daley College, and made the Dean's List and/or Honors List every semester. While attending there, I helped compile a booklet called, "The Inditer," which was composed of prose and poetry written by students attending there at the time. I was able to include a few of my poems, which was very exciting for me. While my poetry book, mentioned earlier, has been published for the general public, my autobiography is being published primarily for friends and family who would like to know more about my life. I also hope friends, family, and others reading my autobiography will see the unlimited benefits in trusting our Lord Jesus with their very life, and follow the guidance of God's Holy Spirit. We are blessed ever so much more when we follow the path He leads us on. However, He only "guides.' He still leaves the choice up to us, to follow Him, or try to handle our life situations "on our own path."

I started Daley College on June 14, 1977, which just happened to be Mom's 56th birthday, and also, of course, Flag Day. One time, when Dad was at work on Flag Day, a newer employee, who hadn't been in the country very long, asked Dad why there were so many flags on display. Dad told him,

"That's 'cause it's my wife's birthday!" I'm not sure if they guy believed him, but we all got a good laugh when Dad told us. Mom really liked that idea!

The same day that I started college, I met Maureen Perazzolo, another student majoring in Accounting. We dated a lot, and studied together. While we we're dating, we made an agreement to avoid eating refined sugar, enriched flour, and any food with preservatives. I also drank no alcohol, although it wasn't part of the agreement. The most difficult part was avoiding food with preservatives, but we did our best. It was a lot of hard work, but I never felt better in my life! I remember my sinuses being really clear during that time. That diet lasted only three months, but it was, I believe, the healthiest three months of my life. I graduated from Daley College in May, 1980, and that was the end of my formal "school-type" education, and also the end of my seeing Maureen. While my formal education ended that day, there's never a day that goes by that I don't learn something. Life is a never-ending learning process!

As mentioned earlier, here are a couple of the poems Priscilla Bedrich and I composed, that were included in the Spring, 1979, 20th Anniversary Edition of the "Inditer." I'll put Priscilla's first, and then include one of mine.

MORNING

Get up, world.
It's morning.
And it's a beautiful time
Of the day.
See the sun
Come up out of its recluse
To greet you
With its lovely aura
Of pink
Yellow
And orange.
This sight helps to wash away
The cares,
Bitter words,
And worries of last night.

Morning always comes along
And cleans the slate
You marked up the day before.
The important things of last night
Are reduced to nothingness
In the morning.
You feel like
There's a purpose to live
And not merely exist.
So take the new, bright day
And make the most of it.

Priscilla Bedrich

ONLY YOU

My life began the day I met you.
I want you so to stay.
There is no way that I'll forget you.
You brighten every day.
The more I know you, dear, the more
I love you, and I know,
My love for you will be most pure,
And it will only grow.

Just knowing I have you, my dear,
I'll weather any storm.
Though there are clouds, it will be clear.
Your love will keep me warm.

Martin L. Dornan, Sr.
To Mary, the Mother of our children

CHAPTER FOUR

1964 – A Year of Decisions

I graduated from Lindblom High School in January, 1964, after attending for 4-1/2 years. Because of my self-consciousness and lack of self-discipline, I was absent from school much more than I ever should have been, and consequently, earned very poor grades in a number of classes. I came to my "better attitude" in my senior year, by changing, and applying myself.

During my last two years of high school, I was working part-time at Dressel's Bakery. When I graduated, it changed from part-time to full-time, and I could have continued my employment there. My goal at the time (not pursued with intention), was to become a CPA (Certified Public Accountant). I really loved accounting and the related fields, but that never came to fruition. I instead, enlisted in the United States Army on July 7, 1964. I got to work in Finance and Accounting (mainly) while in the Army, so I was in the field I enjoyed. When I mentioned to one of my managers, Billy Dressel, that I was going to enlist in the Army, he just kiddingly told me that he was going to go out and buy some Russian War Bonds.

Chronologically, I need to back up about six weeks, because on May 29, 1964, I married Mary (Marylynn Margaret Johnson-Rice). I'll have more to say about her name later. It's really interesting! Since I was only 18, and the legal age for a male to get married in Illinois at that time was 21, I did something very foolish, which will be explained in detail in the next chapter.

It's clear to me now, that my decisions to get married and go into the Army weren't the most mature, to say the least. I didn't counsel about either decision, and basically just did what I wanted to do, and that's my present observation of what happened then.

So, during 1964, I changed from a single, civilian person to a married and "in-the-Army" military person, as a Private in the U.S. Army Finance Corps.

CHAPTER FIVE

My First Marriage

Mary and I met in a local restaurant which I frequented, on the south side of Chicago. Mary's Mom, Edith Rice (born October 12, 1915), worked at the restaurant. She was thirty years older than me, to the day, which I thought was really neat! She introduced me to her daughter, because she said I was such a "nice boy." I didn't fully agree with her assessment, but I didn't argue, either. I liked Mary's Mom, especially since anytime Mary and I would argue about something, she wouldn't just agree with Mary. If she thought I was right, she would tell Mary to listen to me. Anytime she thought I was wrong, she would tell me.

I'll explain some about Mary's full name at the time, Marylynn Margaret Ann Johnson Rice. Her Mom, Edith Rice, wasn't married at the time Mary came into the world. While her Mom knew clearly that Mary's Father was Andrew Henry Jackson, she didn't want to get him into trouble by giving Mary his name (since he was in the military), so she gave Mary the surname of Johnson. Edith's sister, Mary's Aunt Kit, put it into Edith's head that she might get Mary's Dad in trouble if she gave Mary his last name. That's how Johnson became part of her name. And Rice is part of her name, simply because it was her Mom's name, and Rice was on her birth certificate. Mary found out that "Rice" was on her birth certificate when we had to get her a passport in order to travel to West Germany in 1966. She was quite hurt that her Mom never told her about that. I was of the belief that her Dad was a direct descendent of U.S. President Andrew Jackson, but I found out recently that he was not.

Mary (born February 12, 1947) and I dated for a number of months before deciding to get married after I graduated from high school. We were both very young and quite impulsive. Speaking for myself only, I didn't give a lot of thought to the many responsibilities involved in taking that step. I simply did it 'cause I wanted to. I was also not very mature spiritually, and didn't seek any counseling prior to "tying the knot." I asked Mary, "Do you want to get married?" Her response was, "Sure!" So, after that very thorough "discussion," we planned on how it was going to happen, and when. This is one instance where I believe I went onto my own path, and will explain why. I wasn't yet of legal age to get married without parental consent, so I went to the Bureau of Vital Statistics, got a copy of my birth certificate, and rented a typewriter (precursor to word processing on the computer). I then altered my birth certificate to show my year of birth as 1942, so Mary and I could elope, since my Mom didn't approve of our getting married at such a young age. We got married in Carterville, Illinois, in the southern part of the state, by a Justice of the Peace. His name was Lacy Lee, and he had to see the very poorly changed date on my birth certificate, but he married us anyway. As we were leaving his office, he kindly reminded me of the $3.00 fee for his services. A bit embarrassed, I returned and paid him. Mary and I left as a married couple.

As I came from a dysfunctional family, Mary also did. Her Mom was Edith Rice, a single Mom who raised Mary and her younger sister, Kathy, as best as she could. She had never married Mary's Dad. I got to meet him in 1966 when I was in the Army stationed at Fort Myer, Virginia. I worked at the Finance & Accounting Office, right across the Potomac River from Washington, D.C. He was in the U.S. Soldier's Home in Washington, D.C., very sick with pneumonia. He died only two weeks after I met him. The hospital staff must have known that he was dying, as they allowed him to keep a flask of whisky under his pillow. He didn't use it to get drunk. I believe it helped ease his pain. Nowadays, that would be called hospice care. Mary hadn't seen her Dad in many years, and was very blessed to be able to join me at Fort Myer, and see him before he died. The very next day, after seeing Mary, he died. I truly believe he wanted to live long enough to see his daughter. He had retired from the army after twenty years of service, and spent his remaining years at the Soldier's Home. In my book, "Poetry in Emotion - a Christian's Perspective," the poem entitled, "Our Dad" explains the situation a bit further. I'll include it at the end of this chapter. Mary's Mom died a few years after our divorce, and I went with Mary to the wake and funeral, for which she was very grateful.

Our first child, Martin Lee Jr., (Marty) was due on our nine-month anniversary, and came two weeks early, giving the busybodies something to talk about. Mary was living with her Mom in Chicago, since I had joined the Army, and we couldn't afford to rent an apartment to be together.

Marty was born on February 20, 1965. We never called him Junior, as we knew he would hate it when he got older. I was stationed at Fort Polk, Louisiana at the time, and flew up to Chicago to be with Mary, but got there after he was born. He was a healthy baby, weighing in at eight pounds, three ounces, and twenty-one inches long. Marty now has two daughters, Sharlene and Katlin, both living in Illinois, and a son, Joey, whom I believe also is living in Illinois. Sharlene had married Timmothy Raymond Scott Edwards, a gentleman with seven children (four boys and three girls). They then had a son of their own, named Sebastian Zachary Aleister Edwards. His nickname is Noodles. Shar has since divorced Timm, having found out her marriage to him was a mistake, and determined from his actions, that he will not change, and be more responsible. She is raising her Noodles on her own, while Timm and her retain a pleasant friendship.

Marty came to live with me for about seven months (August, 2021 to March, 2022), hoping to find an apartment to be on his own. He just didn't have enough income from his Social Security to find an apartment he could afford. We even attempted to find subsidized housing for him, but even then, the waiting list was insanely ridiculous, like years long. I had driven up to Illinois to bring Marty down to Arizona in early August, 2021, but was unable to drive him back up in March, so he took the Greyhound (with only four transfers!) to Spring Valley, Illinois. His friend Bubba picked him up at the bus station in Peoria, Illinois. Marty left what he couldn't take with him on the bus. I told him that I'd get the rest of the stuff to him as I'm able. Now, with the price of gas over $5.00 a gallon, I'm watching for God to open a window for me to have a way to afford the trip.

Next came Jennifer Mary, (Jenner) was born October 17, 1967. She came to us weighing eight pounds, fourteen ounces, and also twenty-one inches long. She was born at DeWitt Army Hospital, in Fort Belvoir, Virginia, while I was stationed at Fort Myer. I missed her delivery, also. Actually, if I remember right, I was never with Mary for the delivery of any of our children. It wasn't intentional. It just happened that way. Jennifer also has two girls, Elizabeth and Jessica. She is currently married to Larry Denhardt, and they live in Aberdeen, Maryland, which is in the northeast corner of the state, and very close to a large inland waterway. Elizabeth has two children, Alexis Jade and Stephen, Jr. Jessica has a daughter Erika and a son Steven.

Our next baby, Andrew Henry, was born in Stuttgart, West Germany, in June of 1969, at six pounds, three ounces. He was five pounds, nine ounces when we brought him home, very fragile and not healthy at all. He spent most of his very short life in the hospital, and died that September, only ten weeks old. His cause of death was shown as septicemia (a form of blood poisoning), and he died the day after receiving his DPT shot. His body was shipped in a foot locker to Chicago, to the Hank Ketcham Funeral Home, to await our arrival. He's buried in the National Cemetery at Fort Sheridan, Illinois, north of Chicago. I tried intently to investigate his cause of death, but all significant records concerning his death were either lost or destroyed. I understand nothing I could have done would have brought him back, but I was trying to put closure on what actually caused his death. It was very traumatic for both Mary and me, but while my serious grieving was immediate, and Mary supported me, as I got stronger, Mary's grief intensified, and I was able to support her. My heart mainly grieved for his big brother Marty Jr, who at four years old, could only ask, "Why, Daddy, why?" He so wanted a little brother. Jennifer, who was not quite two years old, seemed to take it more calmly, not fully understanding all that was going on, except that "little brother" wouldn't be back. In June of 2019, Mary, Marty Jr., and I went to visit Andy's grave site, and I believe Marty Jr finally put closure on the loss of his little brother. It would have been Andy's fiftieth birthday.

Our youngest child is Laura Margaret, born February 10, 1972, who was the same weight and length as Jennifer, coming in at eight pounds, fourteen ounces, and twenty-one inches long. While their weight and length were identical, their builds were quite different. Jennifer was quite stocky, while Laura was slender, and their builds carried through right to adulthood! I must emphasize here that neither one's build is better or worse – just different. I mention it here only because of the contrast between the two. Laura has four children, Kathryn, Micheal, Jeremiah, and Alex. Kathryn (Katie) has two children, Lisa Diamond, and Willow Wren. However, because of Katie's very young age when Lisa was born, Katie's Mom, Laura, agreed to take Lisa in and raise her. Laura, (Lisa called her Mimi), took care of her until she was seven years old, and then Laura and Grammy Lisa, agreed to transfer custody of Lisa to Grammy Lisa (Lisa calls her Mom). Now, in June of 2022, Lisa is eighteen, and graduated from high school last month. Just the fact that she graduated is an amazing accomplishment for Lisa. Due to the COVID crisis, being unable to attend regular classes, Lisa ambitiously took classes online to keep up her studies, so her graduation wouldn't be delayed. It turned out, when regular classes were resumed, and Lisa asked for credit for the online classes she took, she found out the institution she took the online classes from was not accredited . . . ALL those classes had to be made up, along with the regular classes she was required to take to graduate on time. Lisa did not let that deter her. She worked regularly with her counselor, working to get the classes caught up, in addition to keeping up her regular classes. She even worked part-time at a restaurant for a few months, but found out it was taking too much time away from her schoolwork, which she needed to give more priority to, so she quit her restaurant job, in spite of her manager pleading with her to stay, since she was such a good worker. To make a long story a bit shorter, Lisa completed all the necessary classes, and graduated from high school on May 19, 2022. We're all so very proud of her! She's also a true champion, handling quite well the rejection by her biological Mother (the best that I can tell). I pray someday that the two of them will reconcile, with Katie accepting Lisa as her own.

Micheal was released from prison in mid-January of 2020, and his whereabouts are unknown still (as of June 2022). He called me the day after his release, and told me he would call me again once he got his own phone. I gave him his Mother's phone number, and called and talked with her. That's the last any of us have heard from him. I know he had a probation officer when he was released, but I'm not certain of the length of his probation. I asked his Mom if she could at least contact his probation officer, if nothing else, to at least verify that, if he's still on probation, that he's reporting as required. She let me know he has not reported as required.

Jerry lives in an apartment in Tempe, doing very well for himself. Katie (Laura's oldest child) and her fiancé and their daughter, Willow, had lived there with him for a couple years. For reasons unknown, Katie and her fiance' broke up, and he took Willow with him. Katie left Jerry's apartment to live with a girlfriend she knew from work. Alex has joined the Navy, and is assigned to the nuclear submarine, U.S.S. Toledo, as the radio operator. I dearly love all of them, and pray that Micheal finds a positive path to follow.

Mary and I went through a lot of experiences in our marriage, most especially because of my being in the military, and transferring to different stateside and overseas assignments. It was also a lot of trauma for the children, having to repeatedly leave old friends and make new friends at my next duty station. We did have a number of good times, though, with traveling in different parts of the United States and Europe. In Europe, we were mostly in West

Germany, but we did get to spend one week in Athens, Greece. We stayed at the Hotel Adonis, very near the airport in Athens. We were on the fourth floor, and we enjoyed sitting out on the balcony, watching the passenger jets, which included 747's, landing and taking off from the airport. Mary commented about the food in Athens, saying, "Greece is appropriately named." The food in Athens was very good! However, because olive oil is used so much, it was difficult finding food that would stay on our plate. I would have been assigned to Athens, except for the fact that, due to trauma in his life, Marty Jr. needed special education classes, and they weren't available at that assignment, so I was transferred to Headquarters, Berlin Brigade, in West Berlin, where Marty Jr. got the schooling he needed.

Here is the poem I mentioned earlier in this chapter:

OUR DAD

He's resting now, his soul's now free.
The Lord said, "Son, please come to me."
He prayed just to his daughter see.
And said, "Then, Lord, I'll come to Thee."

His prayer was answered when she came.
They knew each other just by name.
The love that shone was still the same,
Though twelve long years, it went unclaimed.

And then, that night, we did depart.
Dad found no blank spot in his heart.
For then fulfillment played its part.
His soul was free! Whole was his heart!

He said, "Now Lord, with You I'll go.
I've seen my daughter. Now I know
Your love in her will always show.
Please care for her. I love her so!"

June, 1996

CHAPTER SIX

"Thank You" To My Children

It's important that I include a "Thank You!" to Marty Jr., Jenner, and Laura Bunny! All three of you have been more loving and forgiving to me than I deserve. I clearly understand that I've not been the Father (and Dad) I should have been when you were younger. Your Mom left me, and took you kids back to the States while I was stationed in West Berlin, and rightly so! I was much too much the disciplinarian, and not near enough the loving Dad and Father I could (and should) have been. Your Mom was sick and tired of my practicing the teachings of "that church" to which I belonged. And she needed a break from answering all the questions our neighbors had about "that church that your husband practices the beliefs of." I had started practicing those beliefs in 1971, about two years before your Mom left me.

It was a true learning process that I was going through, and your Mom and you suffered because of it. With what I know and understand now, I would give whatever I could to do it all over, and do it oh, so differently! Obviously, I can't, and here's where I repeat, "Thank You!" for your understanding and forgiveness for my imperfections. I love you all very much, and want the best for each of you. I just didn't know the best way to accomplish that when your Mom and I were together. I didn't know how to let each of you be yourselves. My Lord and Savior has helped me immensely to learn His true outgoing concern for each of you. He set the example, and I'm learning daily how to be a better Dad and Father.

Also, if I had it to do over again, I would never have joined the Army. It was just too much trauma for you children, repeatedly moving away from your friends and having to make new friends. A stable home and friends to grow up with is what should have been provided. I say that, because you children had no part in making the decisions any time I received orders to move to a new duty station. I see now many things I should have done back then. I would have gotten out of the military much sooner, had I realized the many complications caused to you children.

I give my humble "Thanks!" to each of you.

CHAPTER SEVEN

The Ups & Downs of Military Life

I went into the Army on July 7, 1964, about six weeks after Mary and I got married. That was another of the "my" path decisions. I could very well have stayed working at Dressel's Bakeries (which became part of American Bakeries Corporation while I was working there), and would have gotten a good wage. Rather than that, I decided I wanted to go into the Army, so I did. I requested to go into Finance & Accounting when I completed the paperwork to go into the Army, and when I got the acknowledgment concerning the schooling I would be taking, it said I would become a "Disbursement Specialist." To me, that sounded like someone working in the Supply Room, disbursing the supplies to the other soldiers. I was a bit embarrassed to find out it had to do with disbursing funds, like Military Pay, which was exactly what I wanted, because I love accounting work.

I took my eight weeks basic training (also called boot camp) at Fort Knox, Kentucky, during the two hottest months of the year. I was assigned to Company D, 14th Battalion, 4th Training Brigade (D-14-4, for short). One time when we were outside during physical training, we all got filmed for the James Bond movie, "Goldfinger." It's in one of the scenes where planes were spraying a "deadly gas," supposedly knocking out all the soldiers who came in contact with the gas, so they (the bad guys) could break in and steal all the gold bullion stored there. The film makers used trick photography to make it look like we all fell down almost immediately after the planes sprayed the gas. No, we didn't get any royalties, but it was cool knowing we'd be in the movie.

Because I completed High School R.O.T.C. (Reserve Officer's Training Corps), I was privileged to be made an acting Sergeant when basic training started. Because of the heat, we often were allowed breaks when we were outside, to sit under trees, while waiting for our platoon to exercise, or fire our weapons. One time, about six weeks into training, while I was waiting to fire my weapon, I dozed off under a tree, not hearing when they called my name to go to the firing range. Needless to say, I became an acting Corporal (one rank below Sergeant). A few days later, something else happened. I don't remember exactly what that was, but I lost that rank, too! While it was a good experience being an acting Sergeant (and then a Corporal), I actually had a lot more friends when I became an ordinary Private, like most of the guys there.

From Fort Knox, I transferred to Fort Benjamin Harrison, Indiana, where I took the necessary classes to qualify as a Disbursing Specialist. Fort Harrison is the financial hub for the Army. At least it was back then. When I joined the Army, July of 1964, the Army's pay system was completely manual, where each military base processed and paid the soldiers (men and women) on that base. Then it became computerized, using the IBM punch card system, and the information was transmitted electronically to Fort Harrison. While it was computerized, there was still a lot of manual work being done to get the pay data ready for transmission. Then JUMPS-Army was developed. "JUMPS" stands for "Joint Uniform Military Pay System", which ultimately became the pay system for all branches of the military. As far as I know, JUMPS is still in use today. The transitions truly had their "glitches," but the overall improvements made the problems much easier to tolerate!

My first permanent duty station, after the training and schooling, was Fort Polk, Louisiana. Mary wasn't able to join me right away, since she was too far along in her pregnancy to travel that far. While I was waiting for her to join me, I attended a non-denominational church for a couple months, but then there was an incident which discouraged me from continuing to attend there. I had invited a Black (now some Blacks prefer to be called African-American) soldier friend of mine to come to services with me, and I happened to mention it to the pastor (Sister Bonner) the week before he was to attend with me. Sister Bonner told me, "I'm sorry, Martin, but he won't be able to attend here." When I asked her, "Why?" she told me, "We southern people have our pride!" I asked her about the two Negro children I saw there, her response was, "That's perfectly fine, because the parents are both White." I found that very discouraging for a "Christian" church to have that very prejudicial practice, so I simply didn't return. I continued going to church, but just went to the chapel on Fort Polk.

I was stationed there when Marty Jr. was born. Being a Private, I didn't have much money, so I asked for, and it was granted, to be excused from my regular work at the Finance Office, in order to take some other soldiers' KP duty, and they would pay me to take it. KP is Kitchen Police, which just means washing dishes, cleaning tables, mopping and buffing the dining room floor after each meal, and other such duties. I took three KP's that next week, each one paying $15.00. The $45.00 gave me enough money to purchase a roundtrip ticket to Chicago, so I could be there for Mary. While I didn't make it back in time to be there when he was born, Mary and I did share some great time together with Marty, before I had to fly back to Fort Polk. Shortly after that, I rented a small house in White's Trailer Court, in Leesville, Louisiana. Mary and Marty then flew down to Louisiana to join me. We had to spray the house and sweep out all the cockroaches before we could move in. Once we did that, we never saw another cockroach in the house. The owners of the trailer park had lived in the house, but then bought a very nice mobile home. That left their house vacant for a number of months before we rented it. It was a nice little house, and it served as our home for the remainder of the time I was stationed at Fort Polk.

I worked in the Commercial Accounts Department at the Finance Office, and my supervisor was a DAC (Department of the Army Civilian). His name was Norris V. Whitaker, and he taught me something which I remember to this day. I often apologized for asking him so many questions, and he told me, "It's better to ask once, than to goof twice." This helped me feel better about asking so many questions. He was the person who was kind enough to excuse me from my duties in the office the week I took three KPs. He was a true gentleman, and great supervisor! I never saw him upset or with a negative attitude.

Shortly before I was transferred from Fort Polk, I lost my wallet. Thankfully, there was no money in it, but I did have to get a new military ID card, driver's license, etc. Except for that, and the incident at the church, the time spent at Fort Polk was most enjoyable.

After being stationed at Fort Polk for about nine months, I was reassigned to the 39th Finance Section, in Hanau, West Germany, (now simply Germany, since the demise of the Wall in 1989). Hanau is about 15 miles east of Frankfurt. Not long after I arrived in Hanau, I received my wallet in the mail. Someone at Fort Polk had found it, and took the time and effort to find out where I was transferred to, and mailed it to me. It was intact. Nothing was missing. I thanked God for that blessing!

When I was transferred to the 39th Finance Section, I first dropped Mary and Marty off at her Mom's apartment, since I had to find an apartment there before they could join me. I had to find an apartment "on the economy," since I didn't have enough rank to qualify for "government quarters." "On the economy" means an apartment or other housing which is not on the base where I'm stationed. "Government quarters" is housing provided to those personnel who qualify for it, and it's normally located on the military base. While I didn't qualify for government quarters, I was authorized to receive a "Basic Allowance for Quarters" (BAQ) which was sent directly to Mary. Because it was such a small amount, the government added $40 to the amount I was allowed, because I was married. Not long after I arrived, I found an apartment in Hanau . . . well, a "sort-of" apartment. It was actually a four-car garage converted into a two-bedroom apartment, which had two wood-burning stoves for heat and hot water. I paid DM220 (that's Deutsche Mark), which at that time was the equivalent of US$55 a month for rent, so it was a great deal for us. We stayed there until we found a better apartment in Gross Auheim, which is only a few miles outside Hanau. This place was actually only part of an apartment. The building was a one-story bungalow, the center of which had been destroyed by a bomb in World War II. The owner simply closed up the inner walls on both sides, and rented them out separately. I don't remember the rent for this place, but we had oil heat and hot running water, which consisted of a miniature water heater by each of the hot water faucets in the kitchen and bathroom. It didn't run very fast, but it was much better than what we had in the prior "apartment."

From Hanau, I was transferred to Fort Myer, Virginia, to the Finance Office. God directed the timing of this assignment, because I got to meet my Father-in-law, (as described in the last chapter), just two weeks before he died, and he was able to also see Marylynn, whom he hadn't seen in years. Fort Myer, being right across the Potomac River from Washington, D.C., is part of the MDW (Military District of Washington). It's also immediately adjacent to Arlington National Cemetery. Mary and the children again went to live with her Mom in Chicago, to give me a chance to find an apartment "on the economy." I still didn't have enough rank to qualify for government quarters. I found an apartment in Alexandria, Virginia, roughly eighteen miles south of Fort Myer. We lived here from 1966 through most of 1968. It was while we were here that Jennifer was born, and a happy time that was! Marty was 2-1/2 years old, and really looked forward to being a big brother. He was very helpful with Jennifer whenever he could be. I remember him picking on her when she got a little older, but he'd immediately defend her if anyone else started to pick on her when he was around, or if she mentioned it to him later.

The Finance Office is just one of the offices located in a three-story building, and I tried working part-time in the evenings, for some extra money. However, with thirteen washrooms in the building, and the time it took to clean them all, it was just too much for me, and the job only lasted two weeks, before I told the Maintenance people I wouldn't be able to continue working for them, and they were very understanding.

We had two very kind neighbors who helped us out anytime we needed it. They were Filipino brothers, Polly and Val Casil. Polly was a Staff Sergeant, and worked at the Pentagon. Val worked at Washington National Airport for American Airlines. Before Polly came to work at the Pentagon, he was President Marcos' (President of the Philippines) personal photographer. It was while he was in this position that he got to photograph and talk with U.S. President John F. Kennedy. Since meeting Polly and Val, I've met many Filipino people, and it seems that their nature is generally most friendly and outgoing – very service-oriented, and not looking for recompense for anything they do.

Another part-time job I found was at the Italian Villa restaurant in Alexandria. It also became too much for me, because I got up so early in the morning to go to the office. I asked if I could work only until 9:00 p.m., and the owner's son told me, "That will be fine!" However, his Father didn't want me leaving before closing, so he told me not to come back. The son took me to the side, and told me, "Come back anyway, and just leave at 9:00 p.m." I only lasted a couple more days doing that. The Father then told me *and his son* that if I couldn't work until closing, then I couldn't work there at all. That time it was final! They were really very friendly people. I got my meals free, and I truly enjoy Italian food!

It was also while I was stationed at Fort Myer that I learned how to drive. When I was very young, Dad told me, "When you can afford a car and the insurance, you can drive." He clearly didn't have any funds to help with that, so I understood. And Chicago's public transportation system was excellent, which helped a lot! For a while, I also purchased a bicycle and rode my bicycle to and from work. I remember riding my bike on Archer Avenue, which was the most direct route downtown. Well, at twenty-two years old, I finally got driving lessons, and bought a car of my own. Before Mary and Marty, Jr. came to join me in Virginia, I was living on base in the barracks (where military personnel live together, similar to a college dormitory, but not as much privacy), and I was talking about wanting to learn how to drive. Steve, one of the guys in the barracks, offered to let me use his car, and he'd give me lessons. I was really both humbled and honored! This was 1966, and Steve owned a 1965 RED Chevrolet Impala CONVERTIBLE!!! And I didn't just learn how to drive, I learned in Washington, D.C. rush hour! Washington, D.C. has very frequent "traffic circles" where traffic from two or more roads meet, and drivers merge into the circle, and then, being in the proper lane, drive off the circle on to the road they're traveling on to. Talk about being nervous! Steve was very patient, and thankfully, I did very well. I didn't even put a scratch on his car. One of the other guys in the barracks had a bronze-colored 1955 DeSoto, which he had just fixed up, and was selling for $250. I purchased it, and enjoyed just driving around. One time, I took a couple guys from the barracks for a ride, and I got on the Baltimore-Washington" expressway. When we got into Baltimore, I came to an intersection where I saw a bunch of route number signs pointing left, but I didn't see any "One Way" signs. To make a long story short, I turned right, only to see six lanes of cars coming directly at us. Thankfully, there was an empty lot immediately to my right. The only barrier was a high curb, which I simply ignored. I went up over the curb and into the lot. The guys with me were laughing hysterically. I think it was out of fear of what could have happened. It couldn't have been because of something I did that I shouldn't have . . . well, maybe. Anyway, we were all okay, and the car wasn't damaged . . . yet. I was so shaken up, that when I went to back up and turn around to get back on the street, I backed up into the corner of a brick building. It didn't hurt the building at all, and it only put a dent in the back, heavy steel bumper of the car. Cars back then had really heavy bumpers, so it didn't do much damage to the car. One nice thing, however, was a junk yard not too far from where I lived, that had two 1955 DeSoto's right next to each other. I also purchased other miscellaneous parts for my car, but not because of accidents, just parts that were old and needed replaced.

My next station was in Stuttgart, West Germany, at the 7th Army Support Command, located at Robinson Barracks. It was in the section of Stuttgart called Vaihingen. By this time, I had reached the rank of Specialist 5th Class (E-5, the same pay grade as Sergeant). That qualified me to bring Mary and the children with me. The apartment we got on the economy was much nicer than either apartment we had in Hanau or Gross Auheim. We were put on the waiting list for government housing, and eventually were able to move there. I enjoyed being much closer to the office. The job I had here was at the 7th Army Support Command. I worked, not in Finance, but in the Headquarters, in an administrative position. I reviewed "Reports of Survey," which basically were reports of government property lost or damaged by a member (or members) of the military. I would make an initial determination of negligence, after reading the statements of the people involved in the incident. I would then pass the report on to a commissioned officer, generally a Captain or higher, who would consider my determination, and then make his final decision. (As enlisted personnel, Sergeants are "noncommissioned" officers, while officers of Lieutenant and above, are "commissioned.") That officer would start the paperwork to notify the personnel involved of the guilt or innocence of their involvement, and the fine and/or punishment, if any. The most common situation involved an individual drinking too much, taking out a jeep, and rolling it (mainly because of the high "center of gravity" of the jeep) by turning too sharply, for whatever reason. They usually ended up paying for the damages, and sometimes the punishment was more severe, because of alcohol being involved. For a long time, I was hesitant to purchase an SUV (Sport Utility Vehicle), because of the similarity they had to jeeps, with the higher center of gravity. However, a few years ago, I purchased a Nissan SUV, and found that as long as a driver is careful and attentive, the chances of rolling the vehicle are decreased drastically.

While we lived on the economy, I would walk to the bus stop to get to work. One home I passed had farm animals in the yard, including a rooster. I enjoyed stopping there for a minute, and mimicking the rooster. He would come strutting up to the fence, and look at me, just daring me to come into "his" territory. God's creatures are truly fun!

There was a gasthaus (tavern) that I occasionally stopped at on the way home, just to have (ein bier) a beer, listen to the music, and then go home. One day the manager came up to me, very kindly, and stated that because of past experiences of Americans getting drunk and rowdy, that Americans are not allowed in their establishment. I started to get up, and was telling him that I don't want to cause any trouble, and that I'd leave. But he told me just to stay there, and he'd go get the owner. The owner came by to let me know it was just fine for me to come in, since I was quiet, and didn't cause any trouble.

I felt good that they would do that for me, and continued frequenting that gasthaus.

We had a very nice experience after we moved into government quarters. Our next-door neighbor had a German maid, and she had a desire to visit her parents in Wuppertal-Barmen, a few miles (or kilometers) north of Frankfurt. Our neighbor wasn't able to take her, and asked Mary and me if we'd be willing to drive her there. We readily agreed. She was a very nice lady, and we had a wonderful time. Her parents were absolutely thrilled to see their daughter, and they treated Mary and me like royalty! We stayed in their home, and ate most of our meals there. If we ate out, they paid the bill. They took us on a tour of their city, and showed us something there that, at the time, was the only place in the world where it occurred. Wuppertal-Barmen has three different levels of public transportation. They have a subway (eisenbahn), which at times is visible from ground level, a train that runs at street level (strassenbahn), and an elevated train (schwabebahn). In one location in the city, all three trains intersect, each at their own level, so they don't interfere with one another. At the point where they intersect, all three are visible to one another. This existed no where else in the world (at that time).

Our little son, Andrew Henry, was born, and also died at ten weeks old while my family and I were in Stuttgart. While this tragedy has been explained in an earlier chapter, I would like to repeat that Mary or myself was always "there" and available to support our other two children through this very sad part of our lives. On the positive side, I look forward to seeing our little Andy in heaven, where he's waiting for us.

Due to losing Andy, I was reassigned to Fort Sheridan, Illinois, where we had the funeral for him. As was mentioned earlier, he's buried in the cemetery there.

I was assigned as a Military Pay Team Chief while stationed at Fort Sheridan. There was one serious difficulty I did have while there. The position I held, in and of itself, was quite pleasant. However, I had a civilian supervisor, who was constantly knit-picking my performance, and virtually anytime I went to this supervisor with a question about procedures, I was referred to another supervisor. Due to my inability to cope with this situation, I requested medication to relieve my stress. The doctor prescribed valium (one pill each morning). Also, because I didn't want to become dependent on the valium, I volunteered for duty in Vietnam. My transfer was approved, and very shortly thereafter, this civilian supervisor was relieved of duty. I will not speculate concerning why that happened, only to say that then, as now, my personality is easy-going and flexible when it comes to dealing with people, and I believe those in charge recognized that, and took appropriate action. I do not say this to pat myself on the back, but only to confirm the extreme obnoxiousness of this person. This was the one and only time in my life that I was ever on medication of this type. I normally took one pill in the morning with breakfast, and that relaxed me enough to cope emotionally with the situation. One morning, and only one, I took two pills, just to see what would happen. Well . . . my feet finally touched the ground about 2:00 that afternoon. I never did that again!! Nor did I ever take muscle relaxers again.

Close to the end of June, 1970, I got two weeks leave (vacation) to be with my family. I then flew to Fort Riley, Kansas for two weeks preparatory combat training. I flew on a commercial jet to Kansas City, Kansas. I continued with a flight to Fort Riley, Kansas in a six-passenger Cessna. That entire (one hour) flight, my stomach had the urge to relieve itself of its contents. I had asked the pilot where the barf bags were. He told me, "Just spread your feet!" It was on this flight that I decided I like 747's a lot better! I think I had divine help in completing the flight without incident.

After the two-week training at Fort Riley, I flew to Denver, Colorado, where I spent the weekend in the barracks of the military hospital. While there, I got a ride to a local Laundromat, so I could have clean clothes for the remainder of my travel to Vietnam. There was a tavern next to the Laundromat, so I went to have a beer. A couple other sergeants saw me sitting alone, and asked if I'd like to go on a picnic to Rocky Mountain National Park. I told them I'd like to, and asked whether they'd wait for my laundry to get done. They told me it wasn't a problem. We then piled into a van belonging to one of the sergeants, and headed out. I don't remember exactly why, but I didn't have any liquor at the picnic, and it's a good thing I didn't. We finally left to go home about two o'clock in the morning, and none of them were sober enough to drive, so they asked me to drive the van. I agreed to, but I only needed one of them to be awake enough to navigate to get me back to the hospital barracks. They agreed, and we were on our way. Well, I was doing just fine, until a squad car turned his overhead lights on, and pulled me over. The street I was on was a multi-lane (each way) road. I was in the right lane, and my navigator said, "Oh! Turn left at this next light!" I looked behind me on the left, confirming it was safe to move over four lanes to the left-turn lane, used my signal, and moved over. I then turned left, and that's when the officer pulled me over. When he asked me why I was pulled over, I told him I wasn't sure. I said I was very careful changing lanes, and then I turned left. He said my lane changing was fine, but I turned left through a red light. To make the story a little shorter, he didn't give me a ticket, since I had my orders for Vietnam with me. That was the good part of this story. The bad part is that when he pulled me over, I was so nervous when I turned off the ignition that I broke the key off in the ignition switch. After the officer left, we found we were unable to get the key out, and we also couldn't start the van. I was close enough to the hospital barracks that I was able to take my laundry and walk there, but the other five guys had to call someone to come and get them. They left the van on the side of the road until the next day, when they were going to call a tow truck. I felt really bad about it, but they took the whole situation in stride. They knew it wasn't intentional, and besides, I was on my way to Vietnam, so they felt bad for me in that respect. That happened on a Saturday evening, and Monday morning, I was on my way to Vietnam. I flew by way of Fairbanks, Alaska and Osaka Air Base in Japan. The plane took me to Cam Ranh Bay, South Vietnam, where I spent my first two weeks for indoctrination. It's fascinating, flying so many thousands of miles west, and crossing the International Date Line. Because of these circumstances, it took me forty-eight hours to fly to Vietnam, but no time at all to fly back home! I got assigned to American Division Headquarters in Chu Lai, (pronounced "chew lie") which is about forty miles south of the DMZ (Demilitarized Zone dividing South Vietnam from North Vietnam). There was a "sapper" attack one night, and the Officers' Mess Hall (dining room) was blown up. One officer was killed, and a few others were injured. A "sapper" is a Viet Cong (North Vietnamese) trained to penetrate the perimeter of our compound, plant an explosive, and then leave, undetected. Most complete their mission, but one was captured shortly before I arrived. Using an interpreter, he agreed to volunteer to show his expertise to arriving American troops, most likely to avoid a trial. His demonstration was most impressive! It was done at night. He was standing on one side of multiple rows of coiled barbed wire, about seven feet deep. When the lights were turned off, in pitch darkness, in about thirty seconds, he was on the other side of the wire, *without a sound*!! He also was without a scratch!

After two weeks in Cam Ranh Bay, I flew on a C-130 to my unit (American Division Headquarters), in Chu Lai. I had flown many times on commercial jets, and wondered why they were called "whisper jets". Once I flew on a

C-130 (cargo plane), I never wondered about that! We could hardly hear ourselves think inside that plane. I never again questioned the term "whisper jet."

We had what we called a "hooch maid," who would come through the barracks each day, doing the cleaning and making our beds. She came by my room one evening after I had returned from the office. She walked up to me, and patted her hand on her crotch, inviting me to have sex with her. I shook my head, "No!" and pointed to my wife's picture on the wall. I smiled to tell her that I was very happy with my wife, pointing to my wedding ring, and continued shaking my head to indicate firmly that I had no desire to have sex with her. To my relief, she finally left. I'm not sure whether she fully comprehended my reasoning for not wanting to have sex with her, but she did leave me alone after that.

I worked in a corrugated tin hut, described as the Finance Office. I was a Military Pay Team Chief. Our "office" was about a quarter mile from a heliport. The double-rotor helicopters would pick up smaller, damaged helicopters, and fly them to this heliport for repair, or disassembly, if they were beyond repairing. Well, anytime they would fly over our "office," our corrugated, tin building would rattle so loud, we had to wait for them to go by, so we could continue our conversation.

I turned out not to be very popular there. A soldier had come in to the Finance Office to see his pay clerk about a problem he was having. He laid his weapon down (which is a serious offense in the first place, and *especially in a combat zone*), and walked a few desks over to talk to his pay clerk. I walked over, picked up his weapon, and brought it back to my desk. When he went to pick up his weapon, I called him over to my desk, briefly explained that his weapon is his "right arm," and that he should *always* keep it on his person, *especially* in a combat zone! I could have had him written up, and told him so, but simply let him go with his weapon and the warning I gave him. He went off grumbling, but hopefully he kept his weapon with him after that! That night, about two o'clock in the morning, someone took revenge on what I did. A tear gas grenade was thrown into the barracks where twenty other sergeants and I were sleeping. We all ran out to avoid the tear gas. Some fans were used to air out the barracks, and about forty-five minutes later, we went back to bed. I really felt bad about what had happened, but did not regret telling the soldier about keeping his weapon on his person. That weapon (about twenty feet from where he was when he laid it down) would have done him no good if the enemy had somehow come into the office and started shooting!

During my stay in Chu Lai, we had one practice alert in the middle of the night. Even though we were administrative personnel, we had to go to the Weapons Room, receive our weapons with ammunition from the Weapons Clerk, and then load up on trucks to go out into bunkers on the beach. The Weapons Room Clerk ran out of ammunition to hand out. The results were that some men wouldn't go out, because they didn't have ammunition, some shared their ammunition, and some men went out without ammunition. Our compound was right along the South China Sea, and our responsibility was to secure the beach front and protect it from attack. The 2-1/2-ton truck (called a deuce-and-a-half) my group had climbed into, had faulty four-wheel drive, so we ended up getting out of the truck and walking faster than the truck could move on the beach. Thankfully, this was only a practice run. I forget how long we stayed in our bunkers before we were allowed to return to the barracks.

I was also able to work for American Express during my off-duty hours, which helped pass the time, and gave me a couple extra dollars for sending back home. I also used it to buy a portable Hitachi AM-FM Stereo transistor radio, with detachable speakers. I still have it today, and it works pretty well. It takes six D-cell batteries, and they last quite a while. I also have an electric cord I can use to save the batteries. I've hung on to the radio, mainly for sentimental reasons, but also because it has very good sound. In 1969, transistors were still fairly new. Transistors replaced vacuum tubes, permitting televisions, radios, computers, and other electronic paraphernalia to be constructed in much smaller cabinets. The miniaturization of electronic parts continues to this day. A couple years ago, I bought a two Terabyte (TB) flash drive, which is the equivalent of 2,000 Megabytes of information, an incredible amount of data in such a small space!! I had purchased two of the flash drives, and gave one to my cousin Phillip, who retired from an IT position with the company he worked for in Chicago. He checked it, and confirmed that it had the capacity, in fact, to hold 2 TB of data!

The American military there had a name for the Vietnamese people, which was "gooks." In English, that means "foreigner." I (maybe not so) gently corrected them, saying, "We're the gooks! We don't belong here!" That went over like a lead balloon. Also, because Vietnamese civilians worked at preparing our food in the mess hall kitchen, they would, very prejudicially, say that "our food was untouched by human hands." I knew I couldn't change their feelings, so I said nothing.

The climate there, extremely hot and humid, caused me to wake up in sweat every morning. We had fans in the office, but they just blew around the hot, humid air. There was never a need for a weather forecast. It was either hot and humid, or hot, humid, and raining. It didn't make much difference to me whether it rained or not, since I was either wet from sweat, or from sweat and rain!

This was indeed a most unconventional war (conflict, officially). Attacks could come from anywhere. A child could be walking by, throw an explosive device, and run. You could "find" a cigarette lighter on the ground, and when you picked it up and went to light it, it would explode. With the sapper attacks, you never really felt safe, even in the compounds, day or night! I'm thankful I never got involved in taking illegal drugs, though I can understand why our personnel would use them because of the uncertainty of where and/ or when an attack might come. I did, however, have my bottle of Old Grand Dad Bourbon. I didn't get drunk, but I would nip on it before going to sleep. I gave what was left to one of my friends when I went back to the States.

Due to circumstances back home, I only remained in Vietnam about a month. The stress of my being in a combat zone was too stressful for Mary, the Mother of our children. She ended up in a psychiatric ward, with the children under the care of another military family until I returned. I believe my being in a combat zone, with the possibility of being killed, so soon after having lost our ten-week old baby, Andy, was just too much for her, and I fully understood. So, I requested and received an emergency permanent change of assignment back to Fort Knox, Kentucky to rectify the situation. It took almost two months for all the paperwork to get processed, so about the end of October, 1970, we returned to Chicago, and I was reassigned to the Headquarters, Fifth U.S. Army Recruiting District, at Fort Sheridan, Illinois. I worked as the Finance Liaison between the Recruiting District Headquarters and the Fort Sheridan Finance & Accounting Office. I was assigned to the Comptroller's Office until April, 1971. My assignment to the Comptroller's Office was necessitated by a personality conflict I had with the Personnel Sergeant and the Warrant Officer assigned over me in Personnel. I won't mention their names, just the situation. The other sergeant had asked me to falsify records for himself and the warrant officer. I refused to be an accomplice in their scheme, and when they completed a required Enlisted

Evaluation Report (EER) for me, they gave me ratings which were clearly below what my actual performance should have been rated. I refused to sign the EER, but rather than press charges against them, I wrote an appeal to Department of the Army (DA), Washington, DC. Also, there would have been no way to prove what happened, as it would have been my word against theirs. To give a brief synopsis of what happened, DA reviewed my appeal, approved it, and removed all evidence of that EER from my records. Had it remained in my records, it would have had a serious effect on my Army career. From there, I was assigned to Headquarters, U.S. Army, Fifth Recruiting District, also located on Fort Sheridan, but I actually worked in the Recruiting Office at 1819 West Pershing Road in Chicago, as their Finance Liaison. I traveled to a number of Recruiting Main Stations (RMS's) in the Midwestern United States with a Sergeant First Class (SFC, which is one rank higher than my rank of Staff Sergeant (SSG)). He would bring the Recruiters' personnel records (201 files), and I would obtain their finance records from the Finance & Accounting Office, and bring them with me. He would stay in the hotel where the conference was being held, and then he'd let me drive his Lincoln to the Motel 6, or other less expensive place to stay. That was a most memorable part of my travels when working as a Finance Liaison.

The Recruiters would come in to their main station, and we'd review their records with them, doing our best to resolve any complaints they may have had, or going over discrepancies in their records that needed correcting. I truly enjoyed helping them get their records straight. Sometimes, it turned out a Recruiter was overpaid, and rather than collect the entire amount back in one deduction, I would help them set up a Debt Liquidation Schedule (DLS), so their debt was collected back over a one or two-year period. The other Sergeant was amused by the fact that, after I was done with setting up a DLS, I would ask them, "Is there anything else I can do for you?" I guess I probably could have thought of a different question to ask them, since I had just told them that they owed the government money from their overpayment. Anyway, that assignment worked out well, since I received an Army Commendation Medal for the work I did while I was there.

It was at Fort Sheridan that I was able to walk just a quarter mile to the office. It was so nice not having to fight traffic, or take a bus. One morning, when I was going to walk to the office, there had been freezing rain the night before, and everything – the street, the sidewalk, and even the lawns, were glare ice.

I started my morning walk to work, and my next-door neighbor offered me a ride. At the first turn, he ended up on another neighbor's lawn, but managed to get us safely to the office. That was quite an experience!

We had a dog named Shadow for a little while, and one time in the dead of winter, I was able to take him for a walk out on Lake Michigan. It was frozen out about fifty or sixty feet from the shoreline. There were certain places I wouldn't go, but the dog was having fun running all over the ice. He really enjoyed himself. We also enjoyed him, until one day, I had him in the car with me. I don't remember where we were going, but it was icy. I was turning a corner on Fort Sheridan, and he jumped in my lap. I was distracted from driving, and the car slid into an "I" beam protecting a fire hydrant. Then when a friend tried pulling my car back onto the road, the back bumper got bent. We then hooked the chain up to the frame of my car, and it came out just fine. I made the immediate decision that the dog would be going to a new home. I took him to the Orphans of the Storm Animal Shelter. It's a place that treats animals humanely, and finds them a home. It doesn't anesthetize them.

One time I had gone to visit a friend who also had government quarters on Fort Sheridan, and went to park by his townhome. I parked in the space next to his, but when I went to leave, I found another car parked immediately behind mine, so that I couldn't get out. I went back to my friend's home and asked him whose car it was. He told me it was his neighbor's car, and that I had parked in his space. I went and asked his neighbor to move his vehicle, so I could leave. He curtly informed me that I had parked in "his" space, and that he was a "Military Policeman!"

I guess I was supposed to be impressed, or something. I simply told him, "And I work in "Finance." He moved his car without saying another word. I would not have done anything to his finance records, but I simply told him that so he would move his car, and so he'd quit being so vain and obnoxious.

While at Fort Sheridan, I told Mary that this was the best assignment I'd had. We had nice government quarters, and I was only one-quarter mile from the office, being able to walk to work if I so desired. All this, and also our being close to Chicago, which allowed us to visit family as often as we had an inkling to do so.

In November, 1972, I received notification that I was being reassigned to Athens, Greece, to the 228th Artillery Group Finance Office. Greece, at the time, was under military rule, and when we got off the plane at the airport, there were soldiers with submachine guns at the ready, to prevent any acts of terrorism. While it was a bit scary, I actually felt very secure. Mary, the children and I arrived there just fine, but only spent a week in Athens. As mentioned earlier, the American school there had no class available for Marty Jr. I consequently received further reassignment to the Berlin Brigade Finance & Accounting Office, in West Berlin. At that time, it was behind what was called the "Iron Curtain." There was a Wall which encircled West Berlin, (because it was located within Communist East Germany), as well as the Wall which separated West Germany from East Germany. West Berlin was like an island of freedom behind communist lines. Since that time, when President Ronald Reagan told President Gorbachev to "Take Down That Wall!", West Berlin has become simply, Berlin, and all of Germany is now simply, Germany! It was a marvelous reunion for many, many Germans when the Iron Curtain was torn down. Marty Jr got the class he needed while we were there.

So, after a week in Athens, Greece, we flew on to Frankfurt, West Germany. The view of the snow-covered peaks of the Swiss Alps coming up through the clouds was a most picturesque sight. We then flew on to West Berlin. There was a very narrow "air corridor" which the Communists (U.S.S.R, or Union of Soviet Socialist Republics) would allow American, British, or French airlines to utilize. We arrived at the West Berlin International Airport just fine. We were met by a driver from the Berlin Brigade Finance Office, who drove us to the Company orderly room, where I started my "in-processing" into the unit. The Personnel Officer was very nice there. Normally, if I came there directly from the United States, I would have had to look for housing on the Germany economy, and then wait for American government housing. While, since I didn't have a permanent assignment between my U. S. assignment and West Berlin, the Personnel Officer showed me as having come from Athens, Greece, even though I was never permanently assigned there. By doing that, I was able to get into military housing almost immediately. They were also very nice apartments. New apartments had been built for the commissioned officers, so we were able to move into the housing formerly used for officers. We spent about a week in a hotel until the housing could be made ready for us.

Part of my two-week indoctrination included a mandatory visit to East Berlin, going through Checkpoint Charlie. That was a place in the Wall (also known as the Iron Curtain, as mentioned earlier) between East and West Berlin, with Allied troops (American, British, & French) on one side, and the Russian troops on the other side. Anyone going through the Checkpoint had to be verified by both the Allied and the Russian troops. We were required to wear our military uniform when going into East Berlin. That and our military ID card were sufficient to clear the Checkpoint on both sides. The scenes in East Berlin were emblazoned on my mind. I almost immediately decided that I'd never return to East Berlin, unless it was again made mandatory. It was very depressing! It revealed the oppression of the citizenry living behind the Iron Curtain under Communism. The buildings, automobiles, people's clothing, and virtually anything else was all black, white, or differing shades of gray. Even the people's attitudes there were depressing (most likely out of fear). Just imagine three women walking down the street, locked "arm-in-arm." As we passed them, none of them said a word, and all three just kept their eyes straight ahead, not even looking at us. While it is understandable, because of the fear-oriented society they lived in, it was still very sad. I never had to go back into East Berlin, thankfully!

The nine months or so that I was there, I remember a couple incidents of East Berliners being shot by the Russian guards along the wall, because of trying to escape to the West. The Allied troops, because of the international agreement, were unable to help these people. Many years later, I was overjoyed when I heard that the Wall, that cursed Iron Curtain, was being torn down.

My time in West Berlin was a very traumatic time for my family and myself. My wife, Mary, was getting very tired of explaining to our neighbors about that "crazy religion" her husband was in. Looking back, I was just trying to abide by the rules the church imposed on its members, under the penalty of loss of salvation. I realized much too late that many of those "rules" were unnecessary. Some were just plain ridiculous! I had initially applied for Conscientious Objector status. That simply meant that I would continue on Active Duty, and go on to retirement. But then, that June (of 1973), Mary took the children to the Personnel Office, and requested (and was granted) permission to return to the United States. This was done without my knowledge. I came home that evening to an empty house. I then found out what had happened. The next day, I moved back into the Army barracks, and arranged for all the personal belongings of Mary and the children to be shipped to them in Chicago. It was also at that time that I changed my request from Conscientious Objector Status to Conscientious Objector Discharge.

That simply meant that I was asking to be released from active duty, rather than stay in the Army as a Conscientious Objector.

Once my family went back to the States, I decided to start attending church services, which happened to be in the Henningerturm, in Frankfurt, West Germany. The Henningerturm is the structure which housed the silos where the grain for Henninger Bier (beer) is stored. Services were held every other Sabbath. The only way I was able to go was to request passage on the Military Duty Train, which traveled overnight between West Berlin and Frankfurt. The reason the train took so many hours overnight (about twelve), was because the American military train was given the lowest priority while travelling through East Germany, and if even a freight train came along, our train had to pull off on a side track while the freight train passed. From the Frankfurt Hauptbahnhof (main train station), I would then catch the local bus to the Henningerturm. Above the silos are three stories of meeting rooms, one of which we used as our meeting place for Sabbath services. There were two ministers, John Karlson and Colin Cato, who conducted the services. Since services were in German, they would alternate who would give the sermon and who would translate into English. Headphones were provided for those of us who did not understand German. Anytime they told a joke, there would be two periods of laughter, one from those understanding German, and following that, from English-speaking members. It was quite fun, as well as very memorable. As I mentioned earlier, services were held every other Sabbath. The first Sabbath I went there was the alternate Sabbath, and there were no services. Before I could leave to go back to the Hauptbahnhof, a gentleman approached me, and asked if I were there for Sabbath Services. I acknowledged that I was, but there were no services that day. Well, he took me out for a steak dinner, and then made sure I found my way back to the main train station. He also came in by train, but he came from Austria. I never did find out his name. God really blessed me that day, even though there were no services.

Concerning my request for discharge, I can recall a few people who interviewed me, or provided character references for me. Colonel Rockwell was the Brigade Chaplain, and after interviewing me, recommended approval of my request. I had many conversations with Specialist 4th Class Reinhardt Boyd, and he gave a very positive character reference. A few other people also gave very nice statements about my character and sincerity concerning my request. Since I was a Staff Sergeant, and could have stayed in the military only another eleven years to retire, they saw my request as honest and sincere.

I started the discharge paperwork in June, 1973, very shortly after Mary and the children went home to Chicago. It was mailed off to Department of the Army, Washington, DC, and came back approved as requested. I was granted an Honorable Discharge. When I was in the process of leaving my unit in West Berlin, a Specialist 4th Class in the Dispensary (Doctor's office) tried to tell me that I couldn't take my medical records until I got my shots updated. His supervising Sergeant heard him, and told him, "Just give him his records! He's getting out of the Army anyway. Don't hold him up for that!" So, he gave me my records, and I left. I flew out of the West Berlin airport early on the morning of September 11, 1973, and was officially discharged from the Army through Fort Dix, New Jersey the following day. Certain personnel at the Fort Dix Transfer Station tried aggravating me, by telling me I had to wait until the following day (the 12th) before I could get discharged. I didn't let it bother me. I knew I was getting out, and I didn't mind waiting one more day.

I got home to Chicago, and went to Mary's Mom's apartment, where she and the children were staying. She came to the front door, and told me she didn't want me back. My older brother, Ted, was single at the time, so I asked whether I could live with him for a while, and he welcomed me cheerfully. It was a response I was glad to hear. It relieved me of a lot of stress, just knowing that I had a place to stay.

While I was in the Army, I received a few medals for performance, and also for accuracy in firing three different rifles . . . the M-1, the M-14, and the M-16. There was also the familiarization firing I had with the 45-caliber pistol. This was while I was stationed at Fort Myer, Virginia, and I had to go to Washington National Airport as the Cashier giving troops funds for their emergency transfer from Europe to Vietnam. While it wasn't qualification, the officer at the firing range gave me his full backing when I fired the weapon. I fired three times at the target, my arm outstretched in front of me. The hole in the target from all three shots was covered with a quarter. I personally thank God that I never had to use deadly force with any of the weapons I fired.

Just one more thing, while my time in the military was very traumatic on Mary and the children, which I still regret, and ask for their forgiveness, I am thankful that God blessed me with the accounting work that I so loved. He took lemons and made lemonade.

CHAPTER EIGHT

In Between & Single

When I got out of the Army in September, 1973, I went to see Mary and the children. They had gone home to Chicago ahead of me by about three months. When I got there, Mary made it official that she wanted a divorce. I told her I wouldn't object, so we went through a friendly divorce proceeding, where I didn't even have to go to court. Once I knew for certain that she didn't want me back, as I mentioned earlier, I went to talk with my bachelor big brother, Ted, to see whether he would share his abode until I could find a place of my own.

It was right around this time that I started counseling with Pastor Carl Gustafson (of the Worldwide Church of God), and he approved my request to be baptized. I felt the need to be baptized again, even though I was baptized at age ten. I now realize the second baptism was unnecessary, but, no harm done.

Ted and I lived together in a basement flat near West 68th Street and South Campbell Avenue (on the south side of Chicago) for a number of months. I remember a humorous incident during my stay with Ted. He and I were sitting at the table having supper, and I asked him to stand up. He asked me, "Why?" I said, "Please, just stand up." So, he finally stood up. Once he stood up, I asked him, "Ted, while you're up, would you . . .?" He hit me (nothing serious), and sat back down. It left both of us almost falling off our chairs from laughing so hard. We remembered that for a long time! Something else we did was very memorable; we bought a bottle of peppermint schnapps, and then went to a health food store and bought a 4-ounce packet of Danish peppermint powder. We then proceeded to mix the powder into the schnapps, and had the most minty schnapps ever!!! We enjoyed it over the next few weeks, a little bit at a time. While it was very good, I've never done that since, and the best I know, neither has Ted.

We moved from there to an apartment at West 47th Street and South Rockwell Avenue (still in Chicago) on the second floor over a restaurant, which would be much better described as a "greasy spoon." The odor of stale grease and overcooked cabbage (kapusta) permeated the apartment, but we rented it because it was very inexpensive. I moved from there when Ted found a sweetheart who lived in Toledo, Ohio, where he ended up moving. I could have stayed in that apartment, but rather used it as an excuse to move. I found a large and affordable 2nd floor apartment at 2667 West Pershing Road, right near the CTA (Chicago Transit Authority) Bus Barns at South Archer Avenue and West Pershing Road. I lived there for quite a number of years, until a lady in my church, Evelyn Kreivis, who lived not too far from me, offered me the rental of the attic of her bungalow, near West 57th Street and South Spaulding Avenue. She was a deaconess in our church. She and her husband Louie owned the house.

I need to take a break here to mention another blessing God gave me when I got out of the Army. Before I came back to the States, Ted, who worked at Crawford Manufacturing Company (pipe hanger manufacturer at West 31st Street and South Kedzie Avenue) as a machinist and truck driver, advised me that the Purchasing Agent was going to quit soon, and asked if I'd like a job there. I responded in the affirmative, so he mentioned me to the Plant Manager, Matt Wagner. Matt talked to the General Manager, Jerry Gardner, and they agreed to let me come in for an interview. I believe it was a Thursday, the day after I got home, that I went to talk with Jerry. He and I talked only a few minutes, and I let him know that I had never held the position of Purchasing Agent before. He said, "That's no problem. When can you start?" I told him I'd be glad to start that following Monday, and he said, "That's fine!" I started out the door of his office, when he asked me to stop by Joyce's desk (the Receptionist) and fill out an application, which I gladly did. That was truly a blessing from our God! I learned a lot in the three years I worked at Crawford. I handled every facet of purchasing there was to perform. I sent out requests for quotes, approved the best quote, and placed the orders. I typed up the purchase orders, distributed the copies, verified the receiving report (bills of lading, etc.) and approved the invoices when they came in. Sales personnel from the companies where I bought material often took me out to lunch, to gain my favor, so I'd purchase their products. I won't say it never influenced me, but I will say I rarely ordered from a company just because their representative took me out to lunch. Matt sat immediately across from me, and one day shortly after I had started working there, I told him, "I never knew I didn't know so much!" Cavanagh, who also worked in the same office, handled the Shipping & Receiving of all the material to and from the dock. On occasion, I would cover his desk when he was out of the office for whatever reason. I always remember Matt and Cavanagh as very dear friends.

It was during this period of employment (September, 1973 to June, 1976) that our United States went into a serious recession. Because of that, our company was having quite a difficult time keeping the accounts payable current. We were running anywhere from 90 to 180 days from the time we got the material to when we paid for it. I remember this time very well! The two suppliers which literally kept our company open were Crown Steel Corporation (a steel warehouse down the street from us), and Delta Screw (fastener supplier on the north side of Chicago). If it weren't for these two companies, Crawford Mfg. would have had to either lay off most of its employees, or possibly close its doors completely. Once the recession was over, I gave the vast majority of business to Crown and Delta, because of their loyalty to Crawford, in providing our needed steel and fasteners, in spite of our not being able to pay for them on normal terms. I personally believe God blessed our company through these two suppliers. Ted had left Crawford and moved to Ohio before I left their employ. The only reason I quit was because I was the only non-smoker in a small four-man office up over the factory., Even with an air conditioner, an air purifier, and the exhaust fan going in the restroom, the smoke was unbearable for me. Management told me there was nothing they could do, so I gave my two-week notice. This occurred before the ban on smoking inside most buildings in the Chicago area. Before I left, I prepared a book of procedures for the new Purchasing Agent to go by, covering every facet of the job I had learned. I stopped by a couple months after I left, and the new Purchasing agent said he was using the book I prepared as his "Bible." He said I was very thorough, and he was very grateful that he had it to use. The Crawford plant closed a few years after I left.

I was unemployed for a couple months after I left Crawford, and then found employment at Campbell Soup Company, at West 35th Street & South Rockwell Avenue. I started out in the Body-making Plant. This is where the cans are formed from flat pieces of tin, and the bottom is sealed. There were either ten or twelve of the machines on the floor where I worked. We had to wear earplugs because of the noise. At full capacity, each of the machines could produce approximately 22,000 cans per hour. While the machines did most of the work, the operators had to be there to stop the machine anytime there was a jam, which seemed to happen often. We'd then clear the jam, get the machine running again, and throw the damaged cans into the recycle bin. Anytime each of us got our machine to operate at a certain capacity, we'd get a bonus for that day's production.

After a few months in the Body-making Plant, I moved into a position in Warehouse Receiving, to temporarily replace an employee who was out on sick leave, and wouldn't be back for a number of months. In this position, I verified the quality and quantity of boxes of soup labels being received. The coloring of the labels was just as important to management as was the quantity. In my eight months of employment at Campbell Soup, there were two things that truly impressed me; the cleanliness of the entire Plant, no matter where I went, and the quality control. It seemed to me they were continually washing down production lines that were between production runs. Their quality control was so strict that if one ingredient was a small percentage off, that entire batch would be pulled from the line, and sold at a reduced price in the Employee Store. It was still good soup, but it didn't meet Campbell's strict quality standards.

Because of my administrative background prior to working at Campbell's, I was offered a job in Human Resources. The only problem was, management asked me to give false information to the State Department of Labor, showing figures that Campbell Soup had at least the minimum number of minority employees in the plant. I could not agree to that, and consequently, did not get the position. Anyway, just looking around, it seemed to me that we had enough of everybody working there. I'm not speaking prejudicially, just matter-of-fact! Mom and Dad taught us as kids to recognize people for their character, not for their race or cultural background. I was laid off a couple weeks after that interview, and when I asked, I was told that I wouldn't be called back to return. I actually remember the date I left Campbell Soup. It was March 4th, 1977, and I *"marched forth"* out the door. A few years later, the Campbell Soup plant moved from Chicago, to consolidate with the Camden, New Jersey main plant.

It was at this point that I decided I had better make something of my life, so I enrolled at Richard J. Daley Community College, at South Pulaski Road and West 76th Street, very near the Ford City Shopping Center. I started classes there on June 14, 1977, my Mom's 56th birthday. I remember in 1978, when I renewed my Illinois State license plates for my car, I got "61477" commemorating the day I started college. It took me until May, 1980 to complete my two-year AAS Degree in Accounting (with high honors), but thanks to the encouragement given me by Priscilla Bedrich, the girl I was dating at the time, I finished.

Getting back to my residences, I lived in the attic of the bungalow on Spaulding for a total of a bit over eight years, from early 1978 through mid-1986. I was there six years when Kem and I got married on May 28, 1983. Three years later, we bought a house at 3347 West 63rd Place, near South Homan. It was an old two-and-a-half story frame home, with a (dirt floor) basement, built in 1899, but it was home to us. Shortly after we moved in, we replaced all thirty-one windows.

Later on, we replaced one of the bathrooms on the first floor. The floor in this bathroom was so rotted, the toilet rocked, and we could see through to the basement without even trying. There were two bathrooms on the first floor and one on the second floor. While we lived there, the two apartments on the first floor were used by Dad (who ended up going to a nursing home the last six months of his life), and Laura and Eric and the children. When Dad went into the nursing home, we let Laura and Eric have the entire first floor. Then in 1993, when we moved to Arizona, they found another place to live. We actually gave them plenty of notice, and they found another place before we moved.

Those last two residences ran from my single life into my married life, so that's all about residences in this chapter.

As I mentioned earlier, Priscilla was my "encouragement" to complete the courses necessary for me to get my two-year degree. I only had two courses left to take to get my degree. She brought that to my attention, and said I'd be foolish not to complete them. I was actually thankful for her motivation. They were related courses, and a good portion of the study work was the same in both classes. She and I also were on the same committee which worked to produce a college publication called, "The Inditer." This publication contained different forms of prose and poetry submitted by students attending the college. She and I were both contributors, as well as workers to assemble and edit the book. A sample of our talents is included at the end of this chapter.

One other girl whose company I enjoyed was Carol Rewocki. She was a divorced, single Mom. She lived in a home on West 70th Place, with her daughter Janet, very near the college. We would study together, and just enjoy sharing our intellect. Sometimes, Carol's ex-husband would come around, and Janet would find ways to get him upset with me, by telling him stuff about me that wasn't true, like," I was being mean to her," when I wasn't doing any such thing. I guess that made her feel special when he would "defend" her.

Another girl I dated at that time was Maureen Perazzolo. She and I studied a lot together. We also took her younger brother and my daughter Laura camping up to Jellystone Campgrounds in Wisconsin Dells. From there, we drove down to Robinson, Illinois to visit my Dad and Norrie for a few days. We went our separate ways after Daley College. The church I was attending at the time turned Maureen off, and at the time, I believed I was doing what was right. Although now, while I'm still a Christian, I have learned that legalism, while it isn't totally wrong, many of the practices are unnecessary, since Jesus' sacrifice has provided the grace we need, and we don't have to worry about being "good enough" for salvation.

I was thirteen years between high school and college, but I finally took that step. I made the Dean's List or Honor Society every semester at the college. I do not say this to boast, but, quite the opposite, to say I finally applied the abilities I was blessed with. When I attended high school, I only made Honor Society in my senior year. The first three years, I was absent much too often, due to excessive self-consciousness, and did not have the proper studying attitude to use my abilities. My actual grade point average (GPA) was 1.997, out of a possible 4.000. That's just confirming that I didn't apply myself to the best of my ability the first three years of high school.

In July of 1978, before I completed Daley College, I decided to start using my accounting talents. So, my last two years of completing my degree were accomplished working full-time and going to school full-time. I found it necessary to drop my schooling down to part-time, and completed my degree in May of 1980.

The job I got was at Roesch & Crosby, Incorporated, a company which was an exporting manufacturer's representative for a number of domestic companies. My employer, the owner and president of the company was Mr. William J. Moore, a very educated man. At that time, he was one of only one hundred people in the United States who held both a law degree and was qualified as a Certified Public Accountant (CPA). Our largest customer was Ladish Company, Tri-Clover Division, located in Kenosha, Wisconsin. They manufactured stainless steel production lines for dairies and certain other food processors. There were a number of smaller companies we acted as exporting agents for, as well, but none had the sales volume we had with Ladish, Tri-Clover. Most of the time, Mr. Moore was a pleasant and generous man to work for. About the only time he gave his employees any difficulty was when his ulcers started acting up, which is very understandable. They were quite painful, and they made his breath almost unbearable. His breath was actually our warning sign to beware, and do our best to respectfully avoid him, as much as possible. Overall, he was a joy to work for, and even though I still had my Dad, he was a lot like a second Father to me. I'd ask him about different situations, and he'd give me his advice on how to best handle them. One year (1982), when I was calling for a rental car to drive up to Wisconsin Dells for our church festival, he told me not to worry about renting a car. He let me use his *red 1981 Ford Thunderbird* for my trip up to the Dells. At that church festival was when Kem and I started dating, and what a time! Our first date was about thirteen hours long!! We went roller skating, garage sale-ing, dancing, swimming, and we went out to eat while I had the oil changed in Mr. Moore's Thunderbird. We went driving quite a bit at the Dells, but I didn't realize how much, until I went to give the car back to Mr. Moore. In less than two weeks, I had put over 1,300 miles on his car, and it's less than 200 miles from Chicago to Wisconsin Dells! Besides giving him the car back with a full tank of gas, I also bought him a carved wooden sword, about three feet long, supported by two brass chains, on another smaller carved piece of wood, both carved and polished very artistically. I was very pleased when he hung it in the office!

Before meeting and dating Laurie Hughes in early 1982, I was trying to find a girl to marry, and then asking God to convert her (to my religion), so we could get married in my church. Needless to say, I was beating my head against a wall (figuratively speaking). It wasn't going to happen that way.

Laurie was a church member, and I met her at a church picnic. A number of years earlier, she had surgery for a brain tumor, but because of the sensitivity of the area, the surgeon was unable to completely remove it. Consequently, shortly after we started dating, it had grown again to the point where it was starting to bother her again. Well, she had decided she didn't want to go through the surgery again, and we found a place in Freeport, Bahamas, which provided natural treatment to stop the growth of the tumor, and possibly reduce its size by dissolving it. The treatment was to take a number of months. I got the money together both for the flight and for her first few months of treatment. She was there for about three months, and due to the tumor having already grown too large before treatment, they were unable to help her. She succumbed to the tumor and died in early August, 1982. It was rather ironic how it happened. We had run out of funds for her to stay any longer at the treatment center, so I was flying there to bring her home, where she'd be able to continue the treatments, but just on a reduced level. Laurie died at about the same time my flight left the Chicago airport. Consequently, I didn't find out about her death until I arrived there to pick her up. I realize now that God has His hand in what was happening, and that He was closing a door. But at the time, I grieved severely! We were planning so many things, and (now) it's over! It is very clear why God says that death is an enemy. It so drastically changes the lives of those who survive! I thank our Lord for the time when "death will be swallowed up in victory!" (reference: I Corinthians 15:54).

So, following Laurie's death, I decided to intentionally seek God's help in finding a potential wife. I went up to our church festival at the Dells, early enough that I was able to put a dozen red roses in three different girls' rooms before they arrived. All three were devout Christians, and in my church. I was asking God for His direction in my life. Two of the girls, both of whom I talked with after they saw the roses, said they had another guy in their life, but they were both quite kind and gracious, thanking me profusely for the lovely roses. Kem and I hit it off quite well, and a couple months after returning from the church festival, counseled with our minister about marriage. Our marriage was consummated on May 28, 1983, which turned out to be one year to the day of Kem's divorce being final. I had been single for about 8-1/2 years.

CHAPTER NINE

A 2nd Marriage – Almost 25 Years

Kem and I dated for about eight months before we got married. This time my potential wife and I counseled with our minister, Mr. Roy Holladay, before making the commitment. We had read an article in "The Good News," one of our church's publications. The article was entitled, "Before You Say 'I Do,' See Page Two." So that's what we did. Part of our counseling included us each making two lists; a list of the things we liked about the other person, and a list of things we didn't like. Pastor Holladay then told us the things we liked are all well and good. It was the things we disliked that he wanted us to concentrate on. "The main thing to remember," he said, "is that we will need to accept (live with) those things we don't like about the other.: He told us simply that we are not going to be able to change the other, and should not get married with a goal of changing the other person. So, we agreed, and set a wedding date for late May the next year. Mr. Holladay also asked Kem if she were willing to marry my family, since I had three children from my first marriage, and my parents were still alive (both of her parents were deceased, as far as we knew at the time). Kem told him she was willing to do this, also.

We held the wedding in my attic apartment (which became "our" apartment) on Spaulding Avenue, with about forty people. We had moved all my furniture out of the front room, having borrowed folding chairs from church to accommodate everyone. Pastor Holladay married us. Rex Bolan played special music on his violin. My brother Ted was Best Man, and the Maid of Honor was our very good friend, Nellie Sheppard. A number of relatives and friends from church attended the ceremony. We followed up with a catered meal at a banquet hall at West 55th Street and South Spaulding Avenue, just two-and-a-half blocks from our apartment.

Following the meal, Kem and I left for our honeymoon. We were headed to St. Louis, Missouri, and on the way, we stopped at Dad's and Norrie's (step-Mom's) place in Robinson, Illinois, for a visit. We never got past Robinson. While visiting there, I had a flare-up of an abscessed tooth. Since I didn't want just any dentist working on my teeth, we drove back up to Chicago to our dentist, Dr. Alvin P. Spiro. Because of the amount of infection in my system, he said Novocain wouldn't do any good. So, for the first time in my life, I had a tooth prepared for a root canal without any anesthetic. The doctor was very patient with me, and extremely kind and thoughtful. He would have me raise my hand anytime I had pain (which seemed continuously), and he would back off a bit. He finally got the nerve out, and *oh*, was I relieved! My whole mouth felt better almost immediately. Of course, it hurt from the! work that was done, but the relief of pressure from the infection was a real blessing! I remember Kem and me going later to St. Louis, and having a good time, but it was not a possibility just then. Dr. Spiro tried for a year to save that tooth, but the infection never completely cleared up. He finally had to pull it. It turned out a good thing that he pulled it, since a cyst was forming at the base of the root, and it might have turned cancerous if not removed.

Kem so very clearly lived up to her word. Being a Certified Nurse's Assistant (CNA) for a number of years before our getting married, she fit right in! She cared for many members of "my" family, which was, and is, "our" family still, even though we're now divorced a second time. It's really difficult being a "step" Mother, or a "step" anything, for that matter. A "step" person is coming from outside the family, or has the task of learning to accept a person coming from outside the family. This, needless to say, creates "step-children." There are so many relational circumstances involved, as to make the process extremely difficult! I know, personally, it took me years, as an adult, to finally accept my Dad's second wife (common-law though their marriage was). For years, I referred to Norrie as, "that woman." Finally, when I matured to the point that I could accept her, we got along great! I need to emphasize here that it was *I* who did the changing, *not* Norrie. She just patiently waited for me to see what I needed to do. At the same time, it made my relationship with my Dad that much easier, as well. I pray continually my children and Kem will have the relationship that Norrie and I had. I also pray they'll still love and accept her, even though we're now divorced again. Siblings who have different parents also have many similar difficulties as "half-brothers" or "half-sisters." I won't go into that! It's all basically about relationships, having a forgiving attitude, and accepting others for *who* they are, and not *what* they are. By "who they are," I mean, "We are all created in God's image – and human – and we all have imperfections." We can have positive-type relationships with anyone we **choose** to, as long as we can have a *forgiving attitude*, or we can choose to be miserable!

I'll do my best here to remember each of the people (mostly "our" family members) whom Kem had been a caregiver for during the course of our marriage.

Before we moved from the Spaulding Avenue address, Kem and I brought Laura to live with us. She had run away from her home with her Mom and step-Dad, Norman, and circumstances dictated the need to change her place of residence and the male adult with whom she had gone to live. Norm, Laura's Mom, Kem and I all agreed that Kem and I would take her to live with us. Even though Laura had run away, Norm knew where she was, and Norm and I went together to pick her up, so she could come to live with Kem and me. Laura didn't think that we would want her, because of her being pregnant, but we immediately let her know that we not only wanted her to live with us, but that we loved her very much, also, and saw her need for help. Laura was sixteen and pregnant, and felt really bad about things that had happened. She was very grateful that we would take her in and love her in spite of all the circumstances. Laura remained with us for the remainder of the time we lived in the attic apartment. As mentioned earlier, we then bought a home on West 63rd Place, where we gave Laura one of the three-room apartments on the first floor. We let Dad have the other one, since he had moved back up to Chicago after Norrie died, and he needed a place to live. He stayed with Uncle Ray and Aunt Marge for a while until we were able to get his apartment ready for him. When he first moved in, he was giving himself his own insulin shots, but then just stopped doing it. That's when Kem took over. She was his caregiver until it was determined by his doctor that he needed constant care.

Between the deterioration of his left foot, and Dad's refusal to stay off it, he ended up needing to go into a nursing home in July of 1991. We would go to visit him once a week. Among other things, we'd walk (with him in his wheel chair) over to the Dairy Queen to get him a treat. Dad wouldn't drink enough water, so he was set up on an intravenous (IV) saline solution. A number of times, he would rip the needle out of his arm. It was necessary for him to go to the hospital to have the IV reinserted. The last time he went to have it reinserted, his heart started giving him serious trouble, and two weeks later, he died. It was in early January, 1992 that Dad left us. The doctor had tried many times within a half-hour to revive him, but I asked them to just let him go.

When Dad went into the nursing home, we let Laura, with her daughter Katie, have the entire first floor. Sometime in the interim, Laura married Eric. I believe Micheal and Jerry were born before they moved from the apartment in our house. They all lived there until Kem and I decided to sell the home and move to Arizona. They found a place to move to in plenty of time before we sold the house. Once we put the home up for sale, we leased an apartment in Berwyn, where we planned to live until we sold the house, and my job in Arizona became available. Well, after we put the $500 down on the apartment, but before we could move in, Automatic Data Processing (ADP) notified us that the job was available in Chandler, Arizona. During the next two weeks, we sold the house, moved all our "stuff" into the garage, so the new people could move in, then packed the moving truck, putting the car on a dolly behind the truck, and headed for our new home in Arizona. We found a widow lady in our church who was able to take over our lease in Berwyn. We were so grateful that she would take over our lease, that we let her use our deposit as her own. That helped her to be able to afford her move into the apartment.

The drive to Arizona took a casual three days. I always tried to park the truck so I would not have to back up, since the car was "in tow" behind it. Kem let me drive the entire distance. She didn't want any part of driving the truck, mainly because we were towing the car. The most fun part of the drive was between Flagstaff and Phoenix, on Interstate 17. It's virtually all downhill, and lots of curves and turns. I took the truck out of "overdrive," so the engine would help to break our speed. That way, I wouldn't have to constantly ride the brakes.

We arrived in the Phoenix, Arizona valley on June 9, 1993, early on in the day. We found a State Farm agent for our car insurance, and then set out to find a place to live. We ended up at the Kon-Tiki Mobile Home Court, at 505 West Warner Road, in Chandler, and found a three-bedroom, two-bath mobile that we liked. It was all the way to the back of the park, and we had a myriad of speed bumps to go over to get to our "new" home.

It was while we lived here that I had my umbilical hernia surgery. In plain English, my belly button was bleeding. It turned out that the place I had the surgery done was immediately across the street from our mobile home park, at the Warner Medical Center. Even as close as it was, I could not drive, or even walk across the street to go home. I had to have a ride home in a car, which Kem gladly did. Whatever happened on that first surgery, it wasn't done satisfactorily. About a year later, I had the same problem, so the surgeon repaired it again. This time it was good. My belly button hasn't leaked again since then. That was about twenty-five years ago.

I went to work in the Easy Pay Division of ADP, in the Chandler office very shortly after we arrived. The Easy Pay Division processed payrolls for smaller companies.

Since we only had one car, and Kem needed it for her home health care work as a CNA, I bought a bicycle and rode it to work and back home daily. There was a shower and locker room at the office, so I was able to take full advantage of it. Before I bought the bike, I had looked into public transportation, but it would have taken over two hours to get to the office, and there were at least two transfers, as well. When we lived in Kon-Tiki, it was a twelve-mile ride to the office. A nice thing about the Phoenix valley is that most of the main roads have a lane on the right specifically for bicycles, so I felt comfortable riding that distance. When there was no bike lane, I stayed to the right, and did just fine.

We lived in Kon-Tiki about fifteen months, sold our mobile home there, and bought another one in the Rancho Tempe Mobile Home Park, which just happened to be in Tempe, at 4650 South Priest Drive. The mobile was a repossession in pretty bad shape, but we got all new carpeting, appliances, air conditioning, and two swamp coolers, among other stuff. By the time we moved in, it was like a brand-new home. My bicycle ride from Rancho Tempe to my office was a nine-mile ride, which I continued while living there.

My employment at ADP got very stressful, as the workload increased. Management was not permitting overtime, and the computer system we were using at the time was very inadequate and time-consuming. I could not keep up the quality of my work to the standard I had learned, so I gave my two-week notice, and quit. Prior to quitting, I had completed applications at about six or seven temporary agencies. Kelly Services was the one that came through for me. They found me temporary full-time work and kept me working until I was able to again find permanent work.

We had wanted to retire in Tucson, Arizona, just a couple hours south and east of Phoenix, on I-10, so we put our mobile home up for sale, found a buyer, and proceeded to rent a nice apartment in northwest Tucson, immediately adjacent to the Foothills Mall. Kelly Services offered me a position right near our apartment at the mall, at the Saks Fifth Avenue Outlet Store. It was just opening up, and needed personnel to take credit applications. I did that for a couple weeks, and then, to stay on with them, they asked me to organize the stock in their warehouse. I did so well that they wanted to hire me permanently, but said they couldn't afford to pay me what I was worth. However, I believe it's because of the "hire fee" they would have had to pay Kelly Services, and not my cost as an employee. The normal fee at that time was three months' salary cost, based on what they would be paying me.

From there, I went to work at FHP, an HMO (Health Maintenance Organization) with their main office near downtown Tucson, so I wasn't able to walk to work anymore, as I did to the next-door mall. All the time I'd been working at a temporary job in Tucson, I continued to look for permanent work, either with FHP or another potential employer, but to no avail. Then one Monday morning, one of the other temps was looking at the want ads, and saw one for "exciting work" up north in Phoenix. It turned out that the "exciting work" was with ADP, and it was the very position I had left when we moved to Tucson. I called the number, and talked with Marcia, my (former) General Manager. I accepted the position, and agreed to start the following week. Having discussed it with Kem, she suggested that she and our granddaughter, Elizabeth stay in Tucson until the end of the school year, which was about four months from that time. That was just one more of the many times Kem showed loving concern toward her "step" family.

I talked with a couple from my church, Barry and Marilyn Fall, (We gave them nicknames of Bear and Mare), who happened to live within walking distance to the ADP office where I'd be working, took us under their wings when we first moved to Arizona in June of 1993, and they've been dear friends ever since. They offered me my own room and bath in their very nice condominium, at no cost. I did help with the groceries while I was there, but they wouldn't take any money for my staying there. I went home to Tucson on the weekends until Elizabeth finished the semester at school. Then Kem and I found a place to buy in Chandler. For a number of years, the four of us would get together on Halloween and go to the mall, so we wouldn't have to be home for the "trick-or-treaters." Neither they nor we believed in

Halloween, so we didn't want to be home when the kids came around. A number of years ago, they sold their condo and moved to Texas to be closer to Mare's family. She informed us a couple years ago that Barry had passed away February 4, 2020. He was a diabetic, and was also on dialysis. He seemed to be stable with his treatments, but took a sudden turn for the worse and passed away. I told her that we grieve with her, and we pray for the Lord to be with her, giving His peace and comfort. We'll always remember Barry for his loving and serving life as a Christian.

I applied a number of times to get a promotion at ADP, even trying to change the division of ADP I worked in, but got no positive results. From the time I returned from Tucson, I worked for another three years at ADP. I found new employment through a friend at my church and took an "Administrative Assistant" position with CDI Telecommunications. This company performed subcontract work for Qwest Communications, locating and repairing residential phone lines when homeowners reported having problems. Most of these repairs involved digging to repair cable that had deteriorated over the years, or that was damaged by other contractors digging in the area, and damaging the phone cable. I was considered part of the staff, even though I wasn't managerial. I was the only staff member who was not a manager. I was there about eighteen months, when business started slowing down. Three months later, our office was informed that one staff member would need to be laid off to reduce costs. Well, since I was the only "non-manager" on staff, Human Resources (HR) determined that I would be the one who would be laid off. Even though the news was unpleasant, my actual departure from the company was quite blessed. I was given two weeks' pay for being let go, and another two weeks' pay when I agreed to sign a statement that I wouldn't sue the company for discrimination. And one more thing – while I only worked there less than two years, and only had about three vacation days unused, which I expected to get paid for, I actually received three *weeks* of vacation pay! I called HR to confirm this was correct, and was informed that it was what they were told. I thanked the HR manager, and hung up the phone. I believe this was another blessing from God for my faithfulness to Him. The funds I received tided me over up until two weeks before I started work at Progressive Insurance, so I only drew two weeks of unemployment checks between the two jobs.

I started at Progressive on August 27, 2001, and took on my first full-time position in Sales. I received eight weeks paid training, and must say

Progressive was the best company I've ever worked for, not only because of the benefits offered, but their flexibility in scheduling made it possible for me to ultimately get "my" ideal working hours, starting very early in the morning, and going home at 3:00 p.m. each day. We still only had one car at the time, so Kem was able to get me to work just fine, and still be able to take care of her clients as a CNA, and then pick me up after work.

The support provided by management was incredible! In my learning process there, my immediate supervisor provided praise for work well done, and those areas where I could improve, I was given gentle correction described as "opportunities." I liked that approach, since it kept even the correction on a positive note. About three years into my work at Progressive, I started getting quite tired at work. I'd go to the company's "Quiet Room," which had recliners and low lighting, to take short naps. That helped for a number of months, but then I started dozing off at my desk, in spite of the naps I was taking. I was already diagnosed with Sleep Apnea, for which I had a CPAP (Continuous Positive Air Pressure) machine, which helped with my breathing while I slept. However, I was having much difficulty adapting to the use of that machine, mainly because of my sinus problems, and my sensitivity to the medications which could have helped me with them. The inability of my body to tolerate the medications, and the fact that I had a perforated left eardrum, caused me not to be able to use the CPAP machine to any great extent. My doctor also diagnosed me with CFS (Chronic Fatigue Syndrome), using the Epstein-Barr blood test, and again my sensitivity to the medications which could have helped were not tolerated by my body. I concluded my service with Progressive on April 27, 2006, and applied for disability insurance through Progressive. Because of complications, and my lack of financial means to go to a private physician to confirm the CFS, I was unable to get the substantiating documents needed for Progressive to approve my request for company disability. I did, however, through the assistance of Caldwell & Ober, a lawyer firm which primarily handles Social Security Disability (SSD) claims, obtain SSD. The final approval of my request for SSD was sent to an Administrative Judge for review, prior to my appearance in court. Well . . . I was truly blessed! The Judge reviewed the paperwork, and she approved my request, without my even having to appear in court. I was simply jubilant!! God really blessed me, giving me favor with that Judge!

I was also able to get partial disability through the VA (Veteran's Administration) for my exposure to Agent Orange while in Vietnam. I developed Type II Diabetes, which is directly linked with exposure to that chemical.

It was about a year or so before I quit working at Progressive that Kem and I stopped attending Worldwide Church of God (WCG). We had a conflict with one of the cell group leaders (I was his assistant). His deceptive attitude toward the Lead Pastor caused us to feel uncomfortable continuing to attend that group. I felt the absence of God's Holy Spirit there. I leave his name out of my autobiography intentionally, and pray that he repented of his rebellious attitude. God only knows, as he has since passed away.

We just quit attending church for a while, and occasionally went to various churches in the area to find one we'd feel comfortable with. In this process, combined with my quitting work, was when our marriage went from "fragile" to "on the rocks." Kem found a completely different spiritual path, which I'll not go into here. I attempted to "understand" it, but it went against the grain of my Christian beliefs.

Kem insisted on ending the marriage, and after two years of praying about it, and hoping for change, I told Kem that if she wanted out of the marriage, I would let her go. As divorces go, it was inexpensive and friendly. We went through the entire procedure "pro se" (Latin meaning "for self"). We did not use lawyers. Kem used a document processing company, which was very proficient and helpful to our completing the divorce. Kem didn't make any outrageous demands in the decree, and it all went quite smoothly. However, while I believe Kem had already divorced me in her heart and mind, and I knew it was going to happen, the actual divorce was very emotionally traumatic for me. I was accustomed to coming "home" to Kem (just two months short of twenty-five years), and when we divorced, I purchased another mobile home down the street from the one we had lived in together. Now I was coming "home" to a residence, void of a wife to share with, and have still never gotten "used" to it, or "liking" it. I've gotten over the "not accepting" part of it, understanding that God has a purpose in all that happens. I just have to learn more of the positive side of being single. In the vernacular, "It ain't easy!" I thank my Lord and Savior for having directed me to a new church home at Mesa First Church of the Nazarene, which is a loving and caring, Christ-centered church. While the church is not a "wife," per se, I at least have a new family I can relate to. While I am a member of Mesa First (now

Journey of Grace Church of the Nazarene – more on that later), I am first and foremost a Christian, part of the body of Jesus Christ.

I was also attending a Men's Bible Study group in the El Mirage Mobile Home Park. The group was started by Rich Sunde, a disabled, retired policeman from Minnesota, whom God inspired to start the group. While it's very small, with six men at the most, at any meeting, I've developed a camaraderie with these men, which creates more "family" for me with whom I can share. This helped me in 2009. At that time, I was hosting the meetings, which stopped during the summer, since the Winter Visitors go home for the summer, and there aren't enough of us over the summer to continue the meetings at that time. Then, in November, 2009, Rich had additional medical problems, including the need for surgery, for which he ended up going to Minnesota to get it taken care of. Our Bible Study group meetings were put on "hold," and eventually just dissolved.

Further update, July 2020: Rich's body finally succumbed to his many injuries and ailments. He passed away, another dear friend gone to see the Lord. I went to his funeral service here in Mesa, grieving with his Father-in-law, Jack Wilson (and many others, of course), who lost his wife in June, 2011, to the ravages of ALS (Amyotrophic Lateral Sclerosis). They were having a second funeral service in Minnesota, and Jack invited me, but I wasn't able to go. There is no cure yet for ALS. It only ends in death, after years of muscular deterioration. It's also known as Lou Gehrig's Disease. Prior to Pam's passing, I participated in an annual Walk To Defeat ALS, with our team called "Pam's Hope", to raise funds for ALS. Since her death, I continue to contribute, and still participate in the Walk, but as an individual, since the team disbanded.

CHAPTER TEN

Denise – Our Unofficially Adopted Daughter

After our daughter Laura divorced Eric, she met and had a relationship with Denise, which lasted for about seven months. When the relationship ended, they remained friends. The end of their relationship was agreed and cordial, overall. Kem and I maintained our friendship with Denise, as well. Denise is very close in age to our son, Marty, Jr.

Because of Denise's lifestyle, her parents rejected her. Because of Kem's and my acceptance of Denise, in spite of her lifestyle, she "adopted" us as her "adoptive" parents. That's why we call her our "unofficially adopted daughter." It's truly an honor to us, for her to think of us this way. Though she doesn't call us Mom and Dad, she does call us Oma and Opa, friendly titles from the German culture for Grandma and Grandpa.

Denise has been a very loving "daughter," with a heart of gold. We've helped and supported her throughout the years we've known her, and she has done the same toward us. I can't count the number of times she's had us over to her place to prepare us a fantastic meal. Most of the time, the meals she prepares are from "scratch!" I consider her a chef, though she denies it. She says, "I'm a detail-oriented cook who wants to know what is in my meals that I prepare." There are times that she doesn't feel like cooking, so she'll take us out to eat.

Because of the recent COVID-19 outbreak, Denise is very protective of Kem and me, but especially Kem, because of the recent surgeries Kem has had. This further strengthens the bond we have with her. However, Denise's anxiety concerning the COVID endemic, and the restrictions placed on the general population, which caused much paranoia, and because of the nature of her employment, the COVID almost destroyed our friendship, as it's been at least eighteen months since we've seen her. Prior to COVID, she had taken us to various museums and aquariums, paying our way.

It's now July of 2022, and about two months ago, Denise needed a driver to take her to the hospital for some outpatient surgery. Because where she worked was so short-staffed, there was no one there who could take off to help her. She called me to ask whether I'd be willing to drive her to the hospital, and then back home, of course. I readily agreed. That was the beginning of the re-establishment of our friendship, a true blessing from God! Denise and I are once again on a loving "Father-daughter" relationship. She also recently has been having emotional problems with her anxiety and depression, and she's been looking all the more to me for support, as her doctor is working to find a proper balance of meds to control her emotional extremes. She lost confidence in one doctor when he took her off a medication that was actually helping her, so she got a new doctor, and he's now working to get the right chemical balance to help Denise.

One of her calming therapies is using colored pencils and color-by-number coloring books, which, when I'm there, I'll color with her, as it's a calming therapy for myself, also. We've also played cards and Mexican train dominoes for the same reason.

Denise knows it may take a few weeks for the doctor to find the right balance of meds to keep her on an even keel. She has some bad days, but she's determined to work with the doctor to get her meds balanced.

Even though Denise is diligently working with the doctor to get her meds balanced, she decided in mid-August of 2022, to resign her position with the Salt River-Pima Indian Community facility. She had worked there for seventeen years and nine months. She told her supervisor that she didn't trust herself going back to work, since her bouts of anxiety might put her fellow worker(s), and herself, in danger of being injured, or even worse. She's 59-1/2, and has applied for Social Security Disability.

I'm thankful for the trust that Denise has put in me, to be there for her to encourage her, or just to hang out. The timing of my retiring in late April, 2022, and her needing me to help her through this traumatic part of her life, was a true blessing from God for both of us.

CHAPTER ELEVEN

Our Friends in Ghana

When Kem and I got married on May 28, 1983, we put an announcement in "The Worldwide News," a periodical that was published by the Worldwide Church of God, and was sent literally worldwide to church members on every continent. In the announcement, we included our mailing address. Very soon after our wedding, we got a congratulatory card from Accra, Ghana, which is in West Africa. Thus began a lasting pen pal relationship with Emmanuel and Rebecca Tettey and their family. Over the years, we have shared many memories, both happy and sad. The greeting cards we receive from them, be they Christmas, Birthday, Thank You, Anniversary, or otherwise, are always very colorful, and often include a picture of a family member. They have also sent us Ghanian shirts, which are quite colorful. They're made of a very light material, quite loose-fitting, and great for the climate here in Mesa.

February is Black History month here in the United States. One February, at the office, all the associates were invited to wear clothing commonly worn by Black people of different countries. My supervisor and I both drew quite a number of comments (mostly positive, but a few not so nice) when I wore one of the shirts sent to me by my friends in Ghana. A few years ago, also during Black History month, I had the opportunity to display some of their unique craftwork (which they had so kindly sent to me), during a luncheon held at my church. It was an honor for me to "show off" their talents. I also had a wall map of Africa, to show people where Ghana is located. Most didn't know.

Over the years, we've sent them a number of items, including a laptop computer (which, because of programming differences, they needed to modify), and a couple compact electronic dictionaries, which could also translate words in about five or six languages. When we could, we would send a little money to help the family through an emergency, or help the children with school supplies. I know there are other things we've sent them, and they've sent us, I just don't recollect what they were.

At the time I wrote my original autobiography, I was retired. I had the time and hoped I could find the funds, to travel to their home in Amasaman via Accra (via simply means a suburb of), to visit them, and learn more personally how they live. Their culture is quite different from here in the United States, and a visit there would help me appreciate the differences.

Over the last number of years, while we still write each other via the postal service (which we now call "snail mail,"), we've been utilizing email communications more frequently. It's quicker and clearly less expensive than regular mail. Even though Kem and I are now divorced, they still ask about her well-being. I let them know also that she and I may be divorced, but I still consider her part of our family. I keep them updated on how we and the children are doing.

It was through our friends clear over in Accra, Ghana (in West Africa), that Kem and I got to write, and ultimately visit, Jim Jarrell, an inmate in an Arizona State prison, in Florence, Arizona, which is about 62 miles (200 kilometers) southeast of the Phoenix valley. Emmanuel and Rebecca were pen pals with Jim. They hadn't heard from him for a few months. When Emmanuel noticed that Jim and I were both in "Arizona," he wrote me and asked if I could contact Jim, to make certain he was doing okay. He gave me Jim's mailing address, and that started up our friendship with Jim. We've visited him a few times, and happy to say, he's leading a Christian life. He's very intelligent, and has been a legal help to a number of inmates in getting their sentences reduced or dismissed. He called himself a "jailhouse lawyer," and kept up on Arizona law constantly. He would find out about changes to the Arizona Statutes, get a copy of it, and handwrite the changes, incorporating them into the Statutes he had already handwritten. For about the last two years or so, he and I were attempting to find an Arizona attorney who would help Jim help himself get an earlier release from prison, due to a Supreme Court ruling that would have been retroactive to the time he was originally sentenced. Sadly, however, Jim recently passed away on May 10, 2022, due to a serious infirmity which caused internal bleeding. He died while the Florence Hospital was getting him ready for a helicopter flight to a hospital which was better able to help him with the condition he had. He was hoping to be a more positive part of society when he was released. I'm looking forward to seeing him in heaven. He's been a true Christian friend, and I've spent a lot of time on the internet helping him with research, since he didn't have internet access to the extent that we in society take for granted. I've also done much typing and mailing of letters to lawyers in our search for an attorney to represent him in his own case. In all that searching, we never found an attorney willing to take on Jim's case. I truly miss Jim and the camaraderie we had.

I let Emmanuel and Rebecca know about their long-time pen pal passing away. They also grieve Jim's passing, and told me they'd pray for God to comfort and encourage me during this time.

CHAPTER TWELVE

Religion and Living Christianity

It is my intent, in this chapter, to give my concept, my understanding of what religion is, as opposed to Living Christianity. Christianity is a way of life. I speak only for myself. If you agree, fine. If you disagree, fine. I am only expressing my view. The reason I include this in my autobiography is because I have experienced both religion and Living Christianity, and they are distinctly different!

I was in a very religious church (Worldwide Church of God) for almost thirty years of my adult life. I want to make very clear that my intent is **not** to belittle any person or group, but simply to explain facts as I understand them. This church was very legalistic, requiring observance of the weekly Sabbath and annual Holy Days, the refraining from eating unclean meats (which can provide one with better health), restrictions on the type of health care received, three types of tithes, and many other "do or should not do" rules to follow. My understanding at that time was that each member's salvation depended upon their full obedience to these rules. There was much love and grand fellowship in this church, and I learned a lot about the Bible, while in this church's religion. I also especially appreciated the teaching from the Bible and the fellowship at the Feast of Tabernacles each year. It was at the Feast in 1982 where Kem and I had our first date, as explained in an earlier chapter. Mr. Herbert W. Armstrong, the Pastor General, was very sincere in his beliefs, and because the membership overall was faithful in following the tithing principles, he was able to travel around the world, meeting world leaders, and helping many countries which needed financial assistance, concerning the welfare of their people. I must emphasize here that the tithing made by the membership was **not** controlled by the church, as it is in a very major sect today. The church would give guidance, if a member had questions about it, but the actual tithing was done in faith by each member.

Due to poor physical health, Mr. Armstrong saw the need to name a successor. He worked intensely with the church's Board of Directors before implementing any changes. In January of 1986, he named Joseph W. Tkach, Sr. as his successor, and instructed him that as God's Holy Spirit directed him to make any changes, to do so. Pastor General Tkach held the office for almost ten years, at which time, he succumbed to cancer. His son, Joseph W. Tkach, Jr. succeeded him, and between the changes implemented by his father, and those he announced to the church membership, our church changed from the legalistic, religious church of the past, to Christ-centered praise and worship, and teaching that Christianity is a way of life, and not a set of rules. Living Christianity is all about improving our relationship with God the Father, Jesus Christ, and the Holy Spirit, as well as with everyone with whom we come in contact. It is also to help others know the love of Jesus, by example, as well as in words. When Jesus asked what the greatest commandment was, the lawyer replied, "Love the Lord your God with all your heart, with all your soul, and with all your strength, and with all your mind, and your neighbor as yourself." And Jesus said to him, "You have answered rightly; do this and you will live. (Luke 10:27-28). Jesus Christ gave His life that each of us (Jew or Gentile) would have, through His gift of grace, the opportunity to live with Him into eternity. Loving Christianity is all about relationships, loving even our enemies! It is not necessary to "like" a person, because many people's personalities, beliefs, or lifestyle may clash with our own; not necessarily right or wrong, just different! We are to show God's love to everyone, because we all have the same potential, and as stated in John 3:16, Jesus Christ died for everyone, *not just certain people!* To paraphrase one principle Jesus gave us, He said, "If you have (or have not) done good to the least of these your brethren, you have (or have not) done it unto Me." The main point is that we improve our relationship with others by having a forgiving attitude toward them, just as Jesus Christ forgave those who nailed Him to the cross (stake, tree, crucifix, etc.). "Father, forgive them, for they do not know what they are doing." (Luke 23:34). By forgiving others for things they may have said or done, that leaves within us more room for God's love to grow, and He gives us a peace we wouldn't know otherwise.

I have found out that Kem was trying to help me, but I wasn't ready for that help at the time. Maybe, in time, we'll get back together, with God's help and blessing.

I never felt "good enough" in the Old Worldwide Church of God, because I was never sure I had "done" enough. Now I know that I have eternal life through Jesus Christ's sacrifice, and by His grace, my sins have been forgiven. I don't have that burden of religion on my back, telling me to be "good enough" for God, so I can please Him. The peace of mind and joy that I now have, I pray that each and every person on Earth would also enjoy. Of course, I have faults, and as long as I'm human, I will have imperfections. But I have Jesus Christ as my Intercessor, and by His grace, I know I'm forgiven.

I'd like to explain my understanding of forgiveness. While one may approach another person who has offended them in one way or another, and offer forgiveness to that person, this is not absolutely necessary. However, if you do offer forgiveness, and they accept it, that can most assuredly help your relationship. Forgiveness, primarily, is a "within-the-self" thing. As I mentioned earlier, when a person forgives another (from their heart, sincerely), the peace of mind given by God for doing so makes more room for God's love to grow within their heart. *True* forgiveness takes away the anger, bitterness, hatred, and whatever other negative feelings we may have toward another person. I mention "true" forgiveness, only because a "convenient, or on-the-surface-only" forgiveness will not remove any negative feelings toward that person. I can give a personal example of forgiveness. I had bitterness toward my step-Mom, Norrie, because I (falsely) assumed that she had taken Dad away from Mom. When I forgave her in my heart, and then talked with her and Dad about it, I found out I was wrong in my assumption. We then became the best of friends! Love and forgiveness work so beautifully in helping people get along!

To re-emphasize, good works are not necessary for us to gain salvation, since we already have salvation once we repent and accept Jesus' sacrifice, thus receiving His gift of grace. Once we have His grace, His Holy Spirit gives us the desire to perform good works for others, and letting His love shine through us to others, that they might desire to have the same joy that we display. The legacy I want to leave my children, grandchildren, and their children, is that I lived a life pleasing to our God, in spite of my imperfections, and that they could do the same toward God, learning and growing in their relationship with our Lord and Savior.

CHAPTER THIRTEEN

My Best Friend, Don

Don and I knew each other from a very young age. I enjoy telling people we knew each other so young, that we talked "womb-to-womb." Our Moms were very good friends. Our apartments shared the same back yard. I lived at 6148 South Laflin Street, and he lived right around the corner at 1504 West 62nd Street. Don was born August 9, 1945, and I was born a couple months later on October 12, 1945.

When we were about seven years old, we'd watch for Don's Dad to come home from work. He had a habit of flicking his partially-smoked cigarette into the grass, shortly before coming in the front door. We would take turns on running out to get the cigarette while his Dad was in the hallway between the apartment house entrance and the door to their apartment. That way he wouldn't see us getting his cigarette. Then we'd run down the gangway to the basement stairs at the back of the house, and alternate puffing on the cigarette until it was too short. By the way, he smoked Camels, which had no filter, and were stronger than most brands. Needless to say, I ended up smoking until I was about 27 years old. When I stopped smoking cigarettes, I smoked cherry-flavored tiparillos (cigarillos with a plastic tip) for a few months, and then stopped completely. Over the next year or so, I recall having maybe a couple "smokes" when I was having a drink, but I could count on one hand the total number of cigarettes I had in that year. My friend Don never quit.

I'll not say I'm any better than Don, but just handled life's challenges differently. As youngsters, we went to church together, but I'm just not sure how much of an effect it had on him. He would want to do things, "cause he wanted to," regardless of his parents' instructions.

He'd ask me to go to a friend's house, and he'd want me to ride on the handlebars of his bicycle. He had a bike, and I didn't, so that would have been easier to get where we were going. I would tell him, "My parents don't want me riding two on a bike, since we might get hurt." He'd then get upset, punch me in the arm, and ride off without me. Then I'd just walk over to the friend's house, meet him there, and it would be like nothing had happened. I needed acceptance by a friend outside the family, and he was that friend, so I put up with his anger and his moods. One day at school, during recess (I was about eight years old), Don and a few of his friends tried to "pants" me (take my trousers off). Well, my arms and legs were just flying all over, and I must have hit one of the guys in the crotch, 'cause he went away limping terribly! Finally, the guys gave up, not having succeeded at their venture. For some reason, they never tried that again. I guess I was too much of a challenge.

Don worked part-time in Queen's Bowling Alley when we were in high school, and by that time, my family had moved to 6222 South Ashland Avenue, just a few doors north of the bowling alley. Well, Don had access to the bar, and he'd go up and drink when the bowling alley was closed. One day he invited me up to have a drink, and I got drunk on vodka and orange juice. He was trying to make time with a girlfriend, but his concern for my making it home distracted him. All I could do was apologize to him over and over again, for deterring him from his escapade. After I got sick in the men's restroom, he made sure I got home okay. My parents were already separated, but that day my Dad was visiting. He was sitting in the front room, and the door to our apartment was at the far end of the dining room from the front room. When I walked in, Dad called out from the front room, "Have you been drinking?" All I said was, "Hm-m-m-m-m-m-m-m-m?" and went back to my room and passed out. He never did talk to me about that evening. I certainly deserved a talking to, and some kind of discipline, as well! To this day, I don't like vodka. I do enjoy a bit of liquor occasionally, but just to relax, not to get drunk or anything close to it. Also, if I'm with friends or family who don't drink, I'll refrain, so as not to offend them.

After our school years, we didn't see a lot of each other. Some five months after high school graduation, I joined the Army, and was in the military for a bit over nine years. During that same time, Don got married, but he was still drinking, and he ended up divorced. He and his wife had a little girl. Anytime his ex-wife dated another guy, Don would get bitterly angry, and he'd tell her that he doesn't want *his* little girl calling any other man, "Daddy!"

There was one time when Don needed a place to stay. It was when I was single and living on Pershing Road. I invited him to live with me, but asked him not to drink at home. He lived with me for about one year, but his constant drinking necessitated my asking him to find his own place to live. The landlord had complained about his drunkenness. I actually ended up moving (to the Spaulding attic apartment), and Don found another place to live. When I packed to move, I found empty vodka bottles all over the apartment.

Don contracted tuberculosis (TB), and had one-third of one lung removed because of it. However, he wouldn't quit smoking, and his drinking was helping him escape from his bitterness and other miseries. The doctor refused to operate on his lungs any further, since he refused to quit smoking. So, with the TB, the smoking, the drinking, and the pain pills he was taking, his body finally gave up. I don't remember the exact year he died, but he was in his early forties. I grieved when I heard that he had passed away, but I was not surprised. He just didn't have the desire to seek the help that he needed. He grieved over losing his little girl to another "Daddy," and the bitterness just kept eating away at him, until his body just couldn't take any more abuse. I look forward to seeing him again, if for no other reason than to say our friendship is still strong.

CHAPTER FOURTEEN

Single Again!

It was in March of 2008, two months short of our 25th wedding anniversary. When, because of irreconcilable differences, Kem asked for a divorce, so I let her go. She had left me in April of 2006, not telling me where she moved to, and not letting any of our friends tell me where she was. After about six weeks, she let me know where she had moved. When I asked if I could move back with her, she said it would be okay. I really appreciated her accepting me back at that time, since it was at this time that I had voluntarily left work at Progressive Insurance because of my chronic fatigue, and I was trying to qualify for disability insurance. I felt like a roomer in "her" home, as she was renting it from a winter visitor while he was up north for the summer, and I had no income to help with the household expenses. The next two years, I prayed that God would soften her heart, and bring her back to the Christian church. I even tried to understand and accept the precepts of where she was attending. I sincerely wanted to attend church together, as we had done for so many years. I was unable to accept the beliefs of where she was attending, and finally told her I would not contest the divorce. I place no blame for the divorce having happened, I just grieve over the fact that we're apart. We're still friends, and we still do things for each other. She cleans my mobile every two weeks, and I'll wash her car, or help her with things around the house. We didn't even use lawyers for the divorce. She didn't make any outlandish demands, so I went along with what she put in the divorce decree.

I was able to purchase a mobile home down the street from the home that used to be ours. I used some of the money from my retroactive Social Security Disability (SSD) payment to buy the mobile on Lot 121. The timing of that payment was a true blessing! Kem stayed in the mobile on Lot 129. At first, she was going to move, and find an apartment. After Gertrude flew out to

New York for what she thought was a vacation, her children told her that she was staying, and not going back to live alone in Arizona. Then, when Kem and her talked about her selling the mobile home, Kem let me know, and I then told Kem that I would purchase the mobile on Lot 121 from Gertrude, to make the transition less stressful for her, and so she stayed.

I thank God for the strength and encouragement provided me by His Holy Spirit. While He has helped me throughout my life, I especially appreciate the help given me since the divorce. My coming home to "just a home," without my wife there has been abhorrent to me. Without God's help, I have absolutely no idea where I would be today, or if I would even **be** here. The comfort, encouragement, peace-of-mind, and joy He has provided have helped me maintain a calm and positive attitude, which I display most of the time. Of course, there are still times I feel discouraged, but I always have Jesus to carry me through, and help me get back up again. "Footsteps in the Sand," by Mary Stevenson (1936) is a favorite poem of mine. I include it here in my autobiography for your perusal.

FOOTPRINTS IN THE SAND

One night I dreamed I was walking along the beach with the Lord. Many scenes from my life flashed across the sky.

In each scene I noticed footprints in the sand. Sometimes there were two sets of footprints, other times there was one only.

This bothered me because I noticed that during the low periods of my life, when I was suffering from anguish, sorrow or defeat, I could see only one set of footprints, so I said to the Lord,

"You promised me Lord, that if I followed you, you would walk with me always. But I have noticed that during the most trying periods of my life there has only been one set of footprints in the sand. Why, when I needed you most, have you not been there for me?"

The Lord replied,
"The years when you have seen only one set of footprints, my child, is when I carried you."

Mary Stevenson (1936)

CHAPTER FIFTEEN

Retirement Ups & Downs

Because of my chronic fatigue, sleep apnea, and other "inconveniences," and because I was falling asleep at my desk at work, I felt obligated to leave the employ of Progressive Insurance. I felt I was not giving the company the proper value for the compensation I was receiving, and it was quite embarrassing to have to ask customers two or three times why they were calling. I was having extreme difficulty maintaining the proper concentration to remember. If it were only one thing they were calling about, I was generally okay. However, if there were more issues, even when I wrote them down, I would often forget to resolve them. Rather than have customers wonder, "What kind of employees does Progressive have?" I took it upon myself to retire and seek permanent disability. While I wasn't able to obtain either short-term or long-term disability from my insurance as an employee of Progressive, I then applied for Social Security Disability (SSD). After a couple appeals by me personally, and with the help from Caldwell & Ober, an excellent law firm which helps with SSD claims, the Administrative Law Judge read the docket, and gave full approval for my permanent disability, stating that there was sufficient evidence of the permanence of my disability. She emphasized that a hearing was not even necessary.

For the first two years, I was very humbled, having to live with Kem, not able to contribute toward the household expenses, since I had no income. She was gracious about it, and never rubbed it in my face, for which I am forever grateful! Then, when the SSD got approved, and I got the retroactive check, I was able to partly make up to Kem for my not having contributed to the household, by paying off a few of our debts. As mentioned earlier, the timing of the receipt of this check was a blessing from God, since it blended in with the obligations in the divorce decree. It made the process smoother for us both. I was also able to purchase a mobile home of my own. Kem had been doing house cleaning for the lady who owned the home I purchased. The lady's children invited her to come out east (New York, I think) for a "visit." Well, once she got there, they let her know they wanted her to stay with them, and not live alone in Arizona. When they put the home up for sale, I called them and arranged for the purchase. If Kem had not been cleaning house for her, I might have heard about it too late. It worked out beautifully, though, and I thank God and Kem for the availability of an affordable mobile home at the very time of my need.

It was July of 2009 at the writing of my original autobiography. At that writing, I had been living alone for about sixteen months. I hated it, but with God's help, I learned more and more how to adapt. My attention span was still not all that great, but by concentrating on a given task, I was able to complete it. Also, I was able to complete a number of smaller tasks. Many times, I would start something, and then go off and start something else, completely forgetting the first task. I had to be really careful if I were cooking or baking anything, 'cause there have been a couple times when I needed to clean up charcoal off of pans. I didn't mind the clean-up as much as I did the smoky kitchen.

Of course, there are advantages to living alone. I don't have anyone to account to concerning where I'll be or when I'll be back, but I'd sooner have someone to share that with, than to come home to an empty house. My prayer (then and now) is that God will either help Kem and me get back together, or that He'll help me find a new sweetheart to share my life with. Needless to say, I'll do my best, with God's help, to follow the Holy Spirit's guidance, and pray that I'll not foolishly go on my own path.

This was the conclusion of my book in July, 2009. It's now July, 2022 . . .

CHAPTER SIXTEEN

Our Marriage Break

A lot has happened since my original autobiography was published. We remained divorced until October of 2015, when Kem agreed to remarriage. This chapter continues with the period of our divorce for that time, which came to about 7-1/2 years.

Picking up where I left off, in July of 2009, with the help of friends, I was able to pick up a couple part-time jobs at different times. I worked about eight months helping a couple in the park with Customer Service at their dry-cleaning shop. Then their store closed due to the combination of fewer customers and a rent increase. Then I got another job at a carwash for a few days a week. That one lasted until I was asked whether I'd like to be a full-time private caregiver for Gerald Myers, an 86-year-old gentleman in my church. I had already been driving him to doctor's appointments, and various other errands. Jerry loved to go out to eat, so virtually every time we went anywhere, he would ask where I'd like to eat. I've never eaten out in my entire life as much as I did with Jerry. I thoroughly enjoyed it! Darlene and Darrell, Jerry's daughter and son-in-law, asked for my services to care for Jerry. This was full-time, for sure! I had to be at their home by 5:30 a.m., when they left for work, and I'd be there until sometime in the evening, ranging from 6:00 to 8:00 p.m., since they sometimes had errands to run after work, or they had worked overtime. I liked keeping busy, so I'd do the dishes, clean the kitchen, vacuum the carpet, wash and dry the laundry, and various other household chores, just to make it easier for Darlene and Darrell when they came home from work. Jerry didn't mind my working around the house, since he was either watching TV or sleeping. Darrell one time told me I'd make a good housewife . . . just kidding, of course. I told him that I live alone and have to do all that stuff myself at home. I had the weekends off, but that many hours a week just wore on me, and after a year-and-a-half, because it was so mentally exhausting, I had to ask them to find someone else, which they did for me. They first had a gentleman from Oregon to help with Jerry, but he didn't work out too well. He assumed he knew better how to care for Jerry than Darlene and Darrell did. So they got their daughter Dawn to care for her Grandfather. For reasons I'm not aware of, she didn't work out either. They weren't sure who next to call, so they talked about it, and said, "Marty!" They called me, and told me they'd be easier on me concerning the number of hours I would be with Jerry. They understood my need to have fewer hours, and they accommodated me. I had about a six-month respite, and agreed to come back.

I then cared for him again, and he also had a Home Health Aide coming in three times a week, to help in caring for him. This is because he was in need of more intense care, since I was last there with him. Of course, we weren't going out to eat, since he was not ambulatory, but Darlene and Darrell always had a good supply of food in the house. I had pretty much free rein concerning what I wanted to eat, but Darrell told me not to touch his Almond Butter, which I acknowledged, and obliged him.

Jerry was quite frustrated at times, because of things he wanted to do, but was unable to accomplish. I told him that God understands. I also told him, "Jerry, do what you can, and if you cain't do it, don't worry about it. God knows what you can and cain't do, and He looks at the heart." He eventually came to accept his limitations, which made it easier to take care of him. I would sit with him while he watched TV. He just loved watching golf. It didn't matter who was playing, and with cable, it wasn't difficult finding people playing a round of golf. I helped with Jerry another six months, and was there when he passed away. Darlene and Darrell were singing him a hymn at the time. He was a true gentleman! I felt honored to be his caregiver. Jerry not only participated in service to the church, he also helped in the construction of the church's Fireplace Hall. He did what he could to help me work with him. In the later months, I even fed him, since he wasn't able to feed himself. I was truly blessed to have Jerry, Darlene, and Darrell as my friends. I still occasionally talk with Darlene and Darrell.

I then applied for work at a number of places, and the one that responded was Walmart, who asked me to come in for an interview. I got accepted at a Walmart Neighborhood store in July, 2014, and worked there until June, 2015. I ventured out into a new field, trying my talents in selling life insurance to small businesses. Well, I fell flat on my face in that field. The gentleman who was training me really wanted me to succeed. He told me I should be enjoying it. When I told him that my stomach was in knots, he gave me permission to turn in my paperwork, which I promptly did the next day. My attempts at that occupation lasted five months, so I did put an honest attempt into making it work. I still cringe thinking about it.

It was during that time that, after much prayer to our Lord, and encouragement toward Kem, that she agreed to remarriage.

CHAPTER SEVENTEEN

Our Remarriage

Kem and I remarried on October 15, 2015, with Pastor Ken Mostue performing the ceremony at Mesa First Church of the Nazarene. Even though Kem wasn't attending church with me, she knew Pastor Ken well enough to ask him to (re)marry us, which he gladly accepted.

Pastor Ken and his wife Linda hosted (and continued to host via ZOOM, due to COVID restrictions) a Monday night Bible Study group in (or from) their home, and Kem still faithfully attended with me. Kem even would go alone many times when I had to work (prior to COVID). However, it's presently July, 2022, and it's been over a year that we've not had the Bible Study, due to Ken's health worsening. He had quit working at Walmart, mostly at Linda's coaxing, because of his body's low resistance to infections and/or viruses. He just a few months ago started back to work for the same people who employ Linda at one of their carwashes.

Since my attempt at being a life insurance salesman was clearly unsuccessful, I applied online for Walmart again, to see whether they'd hire me back, since I left on good terms. The first Walmart store to contact me offered me overnight work as a stocker. I politely refused, and advised them that I just am not cut out for those hours. It would have been 10:00 p.m. to 7:00 a.m., and my "body clock" just wouldn't work right. I had enough trouble handling full-time work during the day, since I'm constantly battling my CFS (Chronic Fatigue Syndrome). While full-time work exhausts me, as long as I stay active, I'm able to put in the eight hours every day. I then went back to the store I was working at earlier, and talked with management. I didn't even have to interview. They agreed to hire me again, and asked when I'd be able to start. That was early November, 2015, and this time, I lasted six-and-a-half years. Fighting the CFS was becoming a losing battle, as my body was becoming much too tired to work, even just two or three hours into my shift. At the beginning of April, 2022, I gave management four weeks' notice of my retiring, and my last day of work was April 29, 2022. I started out in Maintenance, and after six months, I transferred into the Produce Department. It was a bit more pay, but a lot more work. Being in my 70's, I wasn't as spry as I used to be. The work I did, I did well. However, because of my slowness, and not completing the tasks I was assigned, I agreed to return to doing Maintenance. I then took a disability Leave of Absence to have glaucoma surgery. Complications caused my absence to be almost seven months. The problem was not with my eyes, but getting the surgery for my right eye scheduled. The surgeon who performed the surgery on my left eye ended up having to leave the country before being able to schedule the surgery for my right eye. Barnet, Dulaney, Perkins (BDP) then transferred my care to Southwestern Eye, since no other surgeon at BDP was qualified to perform glaucoma surgery. I then had to get new authorization from the Veteran's Administration, to change to a new eye care center and new surgeon.

While I was off work, a new Store Manager was assigned to the store I worked at. He came from Walmart's Corporate Office, a few months before I returned. When I came back to work and saw him, I remembered him immediately. When he had been at Corporate, he and some other upper echelon personnel made a tour of our store. When he saw me, he walked up to me, shook my hand, and started talking with me like he had known me for years! His name was Mustafa. I remembered it, because it's so much like Mufasa (from Lion King). I told Mustafa I remembered his kindness (and his name) from the Corporate visit he had made about two years ago. He was very pleased to hear I had returned to work, since many associates had been asking him when I might be back. He said I was a positive influence among my co-workers. He got me back into Produce, but for payroll budgeting purposes, had me assigned to a Produce/Meat Department role, which I didn't mind at all. I enjoy learning as much as I can. That way, I'm more valuable to my employer. Well, this time, I lasted about ten months in the combined Produce/Meat Department role, and again ended back in Maintenance, since my stamina was not strong enough to keep up with performing all the many tasks which the combined position demanded. And I was again thankful that they were kind enough to keep me working, rather than just firing me because I couldn't keep up. That happened right in the middle of the COVID "shutdown," when many businesses were simply closing. However, since Walmart was part of an "essential" industry, I was able to continue working, while adhering to the health guidelines sent down to us from Corporate. There were millions of Americans, in small businesses especially, who lost their jobs, because their employers were ordered to shut down because of the COVID scourge. Maintenance was spraying the shopping carts multiple times a day, while cashiers and their department managers were using disinfectant cloths to wipe down the terminals where the cashiers and customers touch, going about the checking-out process. Everyone, customers and associates, did their best to maintain "social distancing" (actually physical distancing, since "social" distancing is impossible), which is to stay at least six feet apart from other people. Clear plexiglass shields have been installed in the pharmacy, and by each cashier. All associated were required to wear a face mask. Then in July, 2020, Corporate mandated that all customers of Walmart and Sam's Club would be required to wear face masks, unless they had a medical reason for not doing so. That eventually changed to customers could voluntarily wear the mask, and associates who had the necessary shots would not have to wear the mask. Then we all were able to stop wearing the masks, but people who wanted to, still could wear them.

Kem and I attempted to make our second marriage work as well as possible. However, after almost four years, we have concluded that it still won't work. We're both too set in our ways concerning what society would consider religion. I am a Christian, believing our Lord Jesus Christ died on the cross for our sins, was resurrected from the grave, and sits at the right hand of God the Father. We have the opportunity to accept Jesus as our Savior, and join Him in the Kingdom of God at our resurrection. While Kem and I attended church together for many years, she presently refuses to take communion to accept Jesus' sacrifice. It is my understanding that her current beliefs eliminate the need for communion, and the acceptance of Jesus' sacrifice for our sins. I had prayed for years about this, and continue to do so, and long for the day when we'll be of like mind. My intolerance of our differences about this have generated a second divorce, which was finalized on August 30, 2019. I again agreed to the terms put in the decree, and gave Kem her freedom again. It's very difficult being alone again, after having known her for almost 40 years. I give our Lord and Savior praise and thanks for my relationship with Him. He is my only hope! He strengthens me, helps me "keep going," and I thank Him for every morning I wake up.

Kem and I have remained friends, and I still (and always will) love her with all my heart. I still call her Sparkle, a nick name I gave her shortly after we met, many years ago. I fully understand, that while I can't change the past, I pray Kem will forgive me for foolish comments I've made to her concerning her religion. Our Lord Jesus showed the greatest love a man could have, by giving His very life for each of us, and by His grace, giving us each the opportunity to live forever with Him. God's timing is perfect, and He knows our hearts, and His plan for each of us. In the meantime, I've presented a proposal to Kem regarding her beliefs and mine. "When, and if, we agree to re-marry once again, it will be a private ceremony, unless, of course, Kem would want to invite friends, I'd definitely be open to that! We each will also keep our paperwork for our beliefs in our own room. And we'll not discuss our differences without both of us agreeing to do so.

I foolishly was trying, of my own accord, to convince Kem to re-marry me. Consequently, Kem once again "had too much," and filed again for divorce. I admit it was my own foolishness, and accept full responsibility for Kem's actions. The divorce decree directed, and the court ordered that I pay Kem $500 a month for four years, through the month of August, 2023. Even though I'm not employed full-time, since I left Walmart on April 29, 2022 (having given them a full month's notice), I will faithfully pay Kem the $500 monthly, and add the Clearinghouse fee of $8.00, so she gets the full $500. Since I am paying her at the beginning of each month, I will make the last payment in early August, 2023. I have cut back my expenses (all except one of my contributions) to different charities. I also recently refinanced my vehicle, and reduced my car payment by about $40. I will faithfully pay Kem through August, 2023, as the court has ordered.

We have remained friends, but the Order of Protection has put a "bump in the road" for the time being. I pray that Kem will let it expire after the one-year period it covers, and we can continue being mutual friends. This period without any direct contact with Kem has helped me see, even more strongly, the love I have for her. I plan on continuing our friendship, regardless of our marital status, and in spite of any other person's feelings about our being friends. God has seen me through this most difficult period of my life, and I praise and thank Him daily for that!

CHAPTER EIGHTEEN

A New "Crisis"

Even though Kem has divorced me twice, she and I have remained friends throughout all the ups and downs. Recently, however, she has a neighbor who has befriended her. I have been to Kem's place when that neighbor has been there, or she has shown up after I've arrived myself. Anyway, this woman is an absolute man-hater. I'm leaving her name out of my book, since that is immaterial. Virtually every time this woman and I were both at Kem's place, she would direct a snide or obnoxious comment toward me, or about me to Kem. She told me one time that she's "watching out for" the women in the complex, of course, including Kem. This woman influenced Kem to go to court and get an Order of Protection out against me. She's attempting to destroy Kem's and my friendship. The time period of the Order of Protection is one year. So, for that year I cannot directly contact Kem directly in any way . . . no visiting, texting, email, or any other direct contact at all.

I talked with my lawyer, asking him if I could communicate to Kem through my daughter, Laura. He said that would be perfectly fine, since she's an adult. So, we occasionally communicate through Laura. We text Laura, and simply ask her to "copy and paste" that portion of the text which is for the other party. At first, Laura was hesitant to do it, because she thought she might be considered a "proxy," which may still get me in trouble. But when I told her my lawyer cleared up that problem, she was more relaxed about the matter, and has been faithful in being Kem's and my intermediary. Kem and I both text Laura only when one of us has a question or friendly comment. We don't want to overwhelm Laura with too many texts back and forth. We both appreciate her service very much!

Concerning the Order of Protection, my prayer is two-fold. First, I pray that Kem will not renew it, and second, that Kem will be protected from any further negative influence from this woman. That Order of Protection hit me upside the head like a figurative ten-pound sledge hammer. I went from seeing Kem most every evening after work . . . . to nothing! I'm ever thankful to God for blessing me with the re-establishment of friendship with Boniece. And after I mentioned the situation to Lisa and Grammy Lisa, they told me to come over any time I want to, and I don't even need to call. Also, besides working on my revised autobiography, I've had a couple friends who needed help cleaning, packing, and moving to a new location. God has really blessed me with "things to do" to help me not to dwell on the negative aspect of the Order of Protection.

I fully, in my heart, believe that this Order of Protection will prove to be only a "bump in the road" concerning Kem's and my friendship. That woman was out to destroy our friendship. I pray God will help Kem's neighbor to see the foolishness of her being so hateful toward men, and ask God to forgive her. I personally have already forgiven her, unconditionally, understanding her past as much as I do.

Update: I am very happy to include here that Kem went to the courthouse on September 7, 2022, with Denise going with her for encouragement and support, went before the Judge and had the Order of Protection against me stamped in capital letters DISMISSED, another beautiful blessing!

CHAPTER NINETEEN

Maybe My Last Time Retiring?

After about six-and-a-half years at Walmart, my Chronic Fatigue finally got the better of me. I've been fighting it for years, but recently I started getting fatigued just two or three hours into my shift. I just think, at 76, my body is tired of fighting it. I'm not certain, but I expect Walmart to be my last full-time employer. I may find some part-time work, mainly to ensure that I have the funds necessary to pay Kem's spousal support through August of 2023, as our divorce decree from August, 2019 requires that I do so. I will say that I have no regrets paying Kem the spousal support. I pray that she's putting some of that money away, to help her budget, once the payments stop. Even though she insists on living alone, I still love her, and always will.

Speaking of retiring, there has been a couple changes in the Nazarene church I attend here in Mesa, Arizona. Our Lead Pastor, David Caudle, has retired from the ministry, but he and his wife will both work in administrative positions at our Church Headquarters in Kansas. They are also planning on purchasing their "retirement" home there, as it is very close to much of their family. Our church name has also changed from Mesa First Church of the Nazarene to Journey of Grace Church of the Nazarene, after a very arduous process, with the last hurdle being the IRS (Internal Revenue Service) recognizing, accepting, and officially recording the change. I personally like the name change. While we were the first Nazarene church in Mesa, back in 1959, I feel Journey of Grace is a more appropriate name, as it much better describes our Christian path. Growing in our relationship with our Lord is a life-long process, and His grace makes it possible, since He provides all our needs. By knowing Him, we have the privilege to trust Him and follow His guidance.

I can also add here that after a few months without a Lead Pastor, our "new" Lead Pastor is Pastor Kurtis Strunk. In the past, he was our Youth Pastor, and now we're privileged to have him back! Both he and his family and the congregation are blessed with his return.

CHAPTER TWENTY

And Now . . .?

In spite of Kem's neighbor attempting to destroy our friendship, I will continue to pray for Kem's protection from her, as well as praying for her neighbor, that our Lord will help her see the hatefulness of her actions, and that she will repent of this attitude.

I will continue to look to my Lord and Savior, praying for His help to keep me on His path, following the guidance of His Holy Spirit. I fully understand that the resources available from my God far outweigh anything I could come up with myself. Whatever He has in store for me, I will accept, at the same time striving to live to please Him. It will not be a passive acceptance, but rather one that says, "Here I am, Lord," ever actively seeking His will, ever-striving to be the Christian He desires me to be. The works I am doing are NOT to gain salvation. I have salvation promised to me through Christ's death on the cross for my sins, and His resurrection. The works I do are because I have been promised salvation. Jesus showed the greatest love a man could ever show, giving His very life on the cross for each of us. He came to become human and live a perfect life. He suffered and died for me, and everyone, as it states in John 3:16, "For God so loved the world, that He gave His one and only begotten Son, that *whosoever* believes in Him shall not perish, but have eternal life." And John 3:17 emphasizes his grace toward each and every one of us. "For God did not send His Son into the world to condemn the world, but that *the world* through Him might be saved." God offers His grace, unmerited pardon, to each and every person who ever lived. It is my personal belief, as a Christian, that accepting Jesus Christ as my Savior is the only way to inherit eternal life. No other "path" will provide access to the eternal life offered as a gift to each of us. Satan's desire is to deceive and destroy. "Jesus is the Way, the Truth, and the Life!" (John 14:6).

I will continue to pray for Jesus Christ to return as He has promised (chapters of Matthew 24, Mark 13, and Luke 21"). In George Fredrich Handel's oratorio, "Messiah," my favorite piece is the "Hallelujah Chorus," where it states, in part, "and He shall reign forever and ever . . ." That is my hope, and Jesus is true and faithful to keep His promises. I ask our Lord for the strength and fortitude to affirm my beliefs to any who ask, while I, myself, strive to stay on His path.

www.ingramcontent.com/pod-product-compliance
Lightning Source LLC
Chambersburg PA
CBHW060333130626
46553CB00003B/1004